COMPUTER VIRUSES AND
ANTI-VIRUS WARFARE

COMPUTER VIRUSES AND ANTI-VIRUS WARFARE

JAN HRUSKA B.A., M.A., Ph.D.
Technical Director
SOPHOS Limited, Aylesbury

ELLIS HORWOOD
NEW YORK LONDON TORONTO SYDNEY TOKYO SINGAPORE

First published in 1990 by
ELLIS HORWOOD LIMITED
Market Cross House, Cooper Street,
Chichester, West Sussex, PO19 1EB, England

A division of
Simon & Schuster International Group

Printed and bound in Great Britain
by Hartnolls, Bodmin

British Library Cataloguing in Publication Data

Hruska, Jan
Computer viruses and anti-virus warfare.
1. Computer systems. Viruses. Management aspect
I. Title
658.478
ISBN 0–13–171067–2

Library of Congress Cataloging-in-Publication Data

Hruska, Jan, 1957–
Computer viruses and anti-virus warfare / Jan Hruska
p. cm.
ISBN 0–13–171067–2
1. Computer viruses.   I. Title
QA76.76.C68H78   1990
005.8–dc20   89–77309
                                                     CIP

TABLE OF CONTENTS

To Bozena Bozicek-Ferrari

PREFACE AND ACKNOWLEDGEMENTS

Every chapter I stole from somewhere else ...

Tom Lehrer, in strong Slav accent, singing "Lobachevsky"

This book is about computer viruses which occur on IBM-PC/XT/AT/PS2 and compatible machines running PC-DOS. It does not attempt to deal in any depth with viruses on other machines or operating systems, like the Apple Macintosh or Xenix, although most of the defences and investigative techniques are similar.

The subject of computer viruses is treated from scratch, but basic familiarity with the structure of the 8086 family of microprocessors and their assembly language is assumed. The book provides a framework for discussing a wide variety of virus-related issues:

· How can a virus penetrate a computer ?

· What does a virus consist of ?

· How complicated is it to write a virus ?

· Who writes viruses ?

· How does one protect against viruses ?

· How effective is anti-virus software ?

Apart from procedural advice on how to fight the virus problem, the book also contains the source code of two anti-virus programs: a pattern checker (*SEARCH*) and a fingerprinting program (*FINGER*). Both are written in 'C' (with a few lines of assembly language) and can be used as practical anti-virus tools. For those readers who prefer to buy software, rather than write it, there is also a list of manufacturers of anti-virus software.

A glossary of computer security-related terms is included.

Names such as *IBM*, *Microsoft* and *PC-DOS*, are trademarks, and any name should be assumed to be a trademark unless stated otherwise. Throughout the book, references are made to DOS. Unless stated otherwise, this means Microsoft's MS-DOS (PC-DOS) running on the IBM-PC and compatible personal computers.

The book was created using the *Runoff* text processing package, typeset by *Aldus Pagemaker* on a *Compaq 386/20* and printed on a *Hewlett-Packard LaserJet-IID*.

I am grateful to several people for their help. In alphabetical order **Sophie Cannin**, for her continuing support and stoic patience; **Petra Duffield**, who proof-read the text; **David Ferbrache,** who supplied reference material from Virus-L bulletin board; **Joe Hirst**, whose painstaking disassemblies of PC viruses have revealed so much; **Keith Jackson**, who made several suggestions; **Richard Jacobs**, who wrote the majority of the software featured in the book; **Peter Lammer**, who wrote parts of the text; **Karen Richardson**, who wrote the section 'Creating User Awareness'; **Alan Wear**, who gave advice on the psychiatric aspects of virus writing; **Edward Wilding**, who made several suggestions; and all the others who have attended my talks and seminars over the past two years, asked questions and taught me so much.

J. H.

Oxford, Christmas 1989

1

INTRODUCTION - AN OVERVIEW OF THREATS TO COMPUTER SYSTEMS

Do you think I could buy back my introduction to you ?

Groucho Marx in Monkey Business

When the possibility of computer viruses was first mentioned in 1984, nobody took it seriously. It did not take long before the first wide-scale computer virus infection swept the United States in 1986. This virus infection (by the *Brain* virus) caused a media sensation, but not an outrage. People were genuinely fascinated by the novel concept of a computer virus, but few saw its full dangerous potential. To some people it was not even clear whether computer viruses occurred accidentally or whether they were deliberately written.

One or two reputable computer experts went as far as publicly stating that the existence of a computer virus was completely impossible, and even if it was possible, it would not last very long.

Little did they know ! To date thousands of businesses have suffered from virus contamination. Unlike older viruses (1986/87 vintage) which would place a silly message or a bouncing ball on the screen, new viruses are highly destructive, programmed to format hard disks, destroy and corrupt data. As viral infections become more and more widespread, the danger of damage to data is increasing at an alarming pace.

The virus danger is here to stay. In the USA, the Far East and Africa it has already reached epidemic proportions and it is only a matter of time before it becomes more common in the rest of the world. In just three months in the Spring of 1989, the number of separately identifiable viruses increased from seven to seventeen.

Computer viruses are only one of the many possible forms of attack on computer systems; other common forms are **Trojan horses**, **logic bombs** and **worms**, but since they often occur together, their analysis is important in the context of this book. For example, a virus may often incorporate a logic bomb which triggers on a certain date. Similarly, a virus is often introduced into a computer system attached to a legitimate program, which makes the program an unwitting Trojan horse.

1.1 TROJAN HORSES

A Trojan horse is a program which performs services beyond those stated in its specifications. These effects can be (and often are) malicious. An example of a Trojan horse is the program *ARC513* found on some bulletin boards which pretends to be an improved version of the legitimate data compression utility *ARC*. In reality, it deletes the file specified for compression.

A list containing the names of known Trojan horses was started some time ago and was called 'The Dirty Dozen'. Unfortunately, as it is easy to rename a program, or to write a new Trojan, the list grew rapidly and now contains some two hundred names. It is available on some bulletin boards, but no such list can ever be complete.

Trojan horses are often used as a means of infecting an unsuspecting user with a virus. If a legitimate program becomes infected with a virus, it becomes a Trojan horse and if a user executes it in the belief that he is executing a bona-fide copy, his computer will become infected.

1.1.1 TROJAN EXAMPLE 1: BATCH FILES

The following short batch file, called 'SEX.BAT' is an example of a very simple Trojan horse. **Do NOT try this out, as it deletes all files in the hard disk root directory**. It is worth, however, understanding how it works:

```
DEL <SEX.BAT C:\*.*
Y
```

This sequence redirects the input to the DEL command from the console to the file SEX.BAT which also contains the answer 'Y' to DOS's question 'Are you sure ?'.

If somebody notices this interesting file 'SEX.BAT' on a floppy disk, and simply types 'SEX' to see what the command does, all the files in the root directory of his drive C: (usually the hard disk) will be deleted.

This is an example of a very simple Trojan horse; much greater damage can be caused by skilled, malicious programmers.

1.1.2 TROJAN EXAMPLE 2: ANSI.SYS

The traditional Trojan horse is a program which needs to be **executed intentionally** in order to cause damage. However, it is possible to activate a Trojan horse unwittingly simply by using the DOS command 'TYPE' to display the contents of a text file which contains embedded escape sequences. These escape sequences are intercepted by the ANSI.SYS driver, which is loaded by a command in the CONFIG.SYS file on many PCs, and used by some legitimate software. The Trojan horse writer will often redefine one or more keys on the keyboard. Redefining 'A' as 'S' and 'Q' as 'W' may cause some confusion, but redefining 'd' as 'DEL *.DAT' could have more serious consequences.

This is very easily done. If the following sequence

```
ESC[100;"DEL *.DAT";13p
```

(where ESC is the Escape character, hexadecimal 1B) is incorporated in the file README which an unsuspecting user is invited to TYPE, every time that he presses 'd', the keystroke will be expanded by ANSI.SYS to 'DEL *.DAT' followed by a carriage return. Much more devious schemes can be devised. Bulletin board operators normally scan all messages for escape sequences, in order to prevent unsuspecting readers of messages from picking up this type of Trojan.

The easiest way to combat this type of Trojan attack is to eliminate the statement

```
DEVICE=ANSI.SYS
```

from the CONFIG.SYS file. Many applications today do not use ANSI.SYS escape sequences to output to the screen but call the BIOS routines directly.

1.1.3 TROJAN EXAMPLE 3: THE AIDS DISK THROUGH THE POST

On 11th December 1989 some twenty thousand envelopes were posted in London containing a 5 1/4" floppy disk marked "AIDS Information Version 2.00" and an instruction leaflet. The recipient was encouraged to insert the disk and install the package. On the reverse of the leaflet, in very small print, was the "License Agreement" which requested the user to send $189 or $378 for using the software (two types of "licence"). The Agreement threatened unspecified action if that fee was not paid (*"Most serious consequences of your failure to abide by the terms of this license agreement: your conscience may haunt you for the rest of your life; you will owe compensation ..."*).

Once an unsuspecting user installed the package, the program printed an 'invoice' giving the address in Panama to which payment should be sent: "PC Cyborg Corporation, P.O. Box 87-17-44, Panama 7, Panama". The AIDS package poses as a legitimate program giving information on AIDS and assessing the user's risk group after asking him/her to fill in a questionnaire.

However, the installation procedure makes modifications to the AUTOEXEC.BAT file, with the effect that every time AUTOEXEC.BAT is executed, a counter in a hidden file is incremented. When this has happened a random number of times (around 90) the damage sequence is activated. The user is instructed to wait, while most of the names of the files on the hard disk are encrypted (scrambled) and marked 'Hidden'. The only non-hidden file contains the following message:

```
If you are reading this message, then your software lease
from PC Cyborg Corporation has expired. Renew the software
lease before using this computer again. Warning: do not
attempt to use this computer until you have renewed your
software lease. Use the information below for renewal.


Dear Customer:


It is time to pay for your software lease from PC Cyborg Corporation.
Complete the INVOICE and attach payment for the lease option of your choice.
If you don't use the printed INVOICE, then be sure to refer to the important
reference numbers below in all correspondence. In return you will receive:
- a renewal software package with easy-to-follow, complete instructions;
- an automatic, self-installing diskette that anyone can apply in minutes.


Important reference numbers: A302980-1887436-


The price of 365 user applications is US$189. The price of a lease for the
lifetime of your hard disk is US$378. You must enclose a bankers draft,
cashier's check or international money order payable to PC CYBORG CORPORATION
for the full amount of $189 or $378 with your order. Include your name,
company, address, city, state, country, zip or postal code. Mail your order
to PC Cyborg Corporation, P.O. Box 87-17-44, Panama 7, Panama.
```

This is a typical example of attempted extortion through the use of a Trojan horse. The user is first invited to install the package (which cannot be easily deinstalled) and then blackmailed into paying money in return for safe passage.

Hexadecimal patterns which can be used to search for this widespread Trojan are 4D5A 0C01 1E01 0515 6005 0D03 FFFF 3D21 for the REM$.EXE program ($ is the hexadecimal character FF) and 4D5A 1200 5201 411B E006 780C FFFF 992F for the AIDS.EXE program - see section 7.1.2: 'Scanning Software' as well as the 'SEARCH' program in appendix B.

1.2 LOGIC BOMBS

A logic bomb is a program which causes damage when triggered by some condition such as time, or the presence or absence of data such as a name. A hypothetical example of a logic bomb would be a maliciously modified copy of a spreadsheet which zeroed a particular cell every Tuesday between 10 and 11 a.m., but otherwise did not reveal its presence. The results would be very confusing and difficult to trace.

Several examples of (malicious) logic bombs have been documented. A recent case involved a systems programmer who was writing a payroll package. He decided to 'ensure' his continuing employment by introducing a short sequence of instructions which checked whether his name was in the payroll file. If it was, nothing would happen. But if it was not (as a result of him being fired), files would be deleted and other damage would occur. He was fired, and the logic bomb triggered the destruction. Only after having been promised reinstatement by the employer did he agree to point out the logic bomb in the code. He was not prosecuted.

Another example of logic bombs happened at IBM. At 7:30 a.m. on 11th April 1980 all IBM 4341s stopped dead. The problem was eventually traced to a logic bomb triggered on that date (i.e. a time bomb), which was placed in software by a disgruntled employee.

Logic bombs are often found in viruses, where the payload is triggered when a certain condition is met. For example, the *Cascade* virus produced its side-effects only between 1st October 1988 and 31st December 1988. The *Datacrime* virus formats hard disks between 13th October and 31st December of any year. The *Italian* virus puts the bouncing ball on the screen only if a disk access is made during a 2-second interval every 30 minutes. The delay due to the logic bomb allows the virus to spread unnoticed, and show its side-effects after it has reproduced extensively.

1.3 VIRUSES

Computer viruses (and worms) are best defined by four essential characteristics:

1. Replication: Viruses make copies of themselves, spreading across floppy disks, computer systems and networks. This similarity with their biological counterparts has given viruses their name.

2. Executable path: **For a virus to do anything, it must be executed.** This normally occurs in a parasitic way, so that the user is not aware that the virus has been executed. The operating system, which is executed automatically on startup, or commonly executed applications, are both, from the virus' point of view, good 'vehicles' on which to hitch a free ride. To do this, a virus needs to make some modification to the program involved. The extent of this modification can be surprisingly small.

3. Side-effects: Viruses do not normally consist only of self-replicating code; they also contain a '**payload**'. This is comparable to a missile carrying a warhead; the self-replicating code is analogous to the missile and the side-effects to the warhead. It is easy to program the payload side-effects to be malicious.

4. Disguise: The successful spread of a virus depends on how long it can replicate unnoticed, before its presence is made known by the activation of side-effects. Replicating longevity is achieved through two methods of disguise - encryption (scrambling) and interrupt interception. These are described in section 3.3: 'Virus Hiding Mechanisms'.

The above characteristics are discussed in greater detail in later chapters. For examples of viruses see chapter 4: 'Common IBM PC viruses'.

1.4 WORMS

Worms are similar to viruses, but unlike viruses (which need a carrier in order to replicate), worms replicate in their entirety, creating exact copies of themselves. Worms are normally found on computer networks and multi-user computers, and use inter-computer or inter-user communications as the transmission medium.

1.4.1 WORM EXAMPLE 1: CHRISTMAS TREE ON IBM VM

Probably the best known mainframe worm was the *Christmas Tree worm* which paralysed the IBM worldwide network on 25th December 1987.

The *Christmas Tree worm* is written in EXEC and can spread on VM/CMS installations. The program is a combination of a Trojan horse and a chain letter. It invites the user to type 'CHRISTMAS', draws a Christmas tree on user terminals and sends itself to all the user's correspondents in the user files NAMES and NETLOG.

```
                *
                *
              * * *
             * * * * *
            * * * * * *
           * * * * * * * *
         * * * * * * * * * * *
            * * * * * *
           * * * * * * * * *
         * * * * * * * * * * *
       * * * * * * * * * * * * * *
          * * * * * * * * *
         * * * * * * * * * * *
       * * * * * * * * * * * * * *
     * * * * * * * * * * * * * * * * *
       * * * * * * * * * * * * *
      * * * * * * * * * * * * * *
    * * * * * * * * * * * * * * * * * *
  * * * * * * * * * * * * * * * * * * * *
             * * * * * *
             * * * * * *
             * * * * * *
```

1.4.2 WORM EXAMPLE 2: INTERNET WORM ON UNIX

A number of widely publicised worm attacks have occurred on Unix systems. The most widely reported attack was the Internet worm which struck the US DARPA Internet computer network on 2nd November 1988. The worm was allegedly released by Robert T. Morris, a Cornell University student. The worm replicated by exploiting a number of bugs in the Unix operating system running on VAX and Sun Microsystems hardware, including a bug in *sendmail* (an electronic mail program) and in *fingerd* (a program for getting details of who is logged in). Stanford University, Massachusetts Institute of Technology, the University of Maryland and Berkeley University were infected within 5 hours of the worm being released. The NASA Research Institute at Ames and the Lawrence Livermore National Laboratory were also infected. The UK was unaffected.

The worm consisted of some 4000 lines of 'C' code and once it was decompiled, the specialists distributed bug fixes to *sendmail* and *fingerd*, which prevented further spreading. From the decompilation, it appears that the worm was not malicious. It did, however, cause the overloading of infected systems.

1.4.3 WORM EXAMPLE 3: SPAN WORM ON VAX/VMS

On 16th October 1989 VAX/VMS computers on the SPAN network were attacked by a worm. The worm propagated via DECnet protocols and if it discovered that it was running with system privileges, it changed the system announcement message to:

```
W O R M S   A G A I N S T   N U C L E A R   K I L L E R S
```

An abbreviated form of this message was then presented in graphics, followed by

```
"You talk of times of peace for all, and then prepare for
war".
```

The worm also changed the DECNET account password to a random string and mailed the information on the password to the user GEMPAK on SPAN node 6.59. If the worm had system privileges, it disabled mail to the SYSTEM account and modified the system login command procedure to *appear* to delete all files (it didn't actually do it). The worm then proceeded to access other systems by picking node numbers at random and used the PHONE command to get a list of active users on the remote system. After accessing the RIGHTSLIST file, it attempted to access the remote system using the list of users found, to which it added a list of 81 standard users coded into the worm. It penetrated accounts where passwords were the same as the name of the account or were null.

The worm then looked for an account which had access to SYSUAF.DAT. If such an account was found, the worm copied itself to that account and started executing.

Within a very short time, the Computer Emergency Response Team (CERT) in the USA (Telephone 412-268-7090) issued a warning and the corrective response.

2

HOW CAN A VIRUS PENETRATE A COMPUTER ?

*"Out of sight, out of mind" when translated into Russian
and back by computer became "Invisible maniac"*

A. Calder-Marshall, Listener, 23 April 1964

There is nothing magic about the way a virus penetrates a computer. The methods of entry are well understood and taking them into account when using a PC is the first step towards combating the virus threat.

2.1 INFECTED PC AND INFECTED MEDIUM

It is very important to distinguish between an *infected PC* and an *infected medium*. The PC becomes infected when virus code is executed and switching off the PC clears the virus from the PC memory. Most media infected with a virus, however, will carry the virus even after power failure.

For example, if a PC becomes infected with the *Italian* virus from a floppy disk, the hard disk will also become infected. If the power is switched off, the virus will disappear from the PC memory, but **not** from the hard disk. When the power is switched on and the PC bootstrapped (started) from the hard disk, it will, again, become infected.

2.2 EXECUTABLE PATH

In order to penetrate a computer, a virus must be given a chance to execute. Since executable objects on a PC are known, **all virus attack points can be listed**. By making sure that the system executes only legitimate, virus-free code, the system will be protected from infection.

In addition to the obvious executable files like COM and EXE programs, **any file which contains executable code** has to be treated as a potential virus carrier. This includes files with interpreted BASIC commands, spreadsheet macros etc.

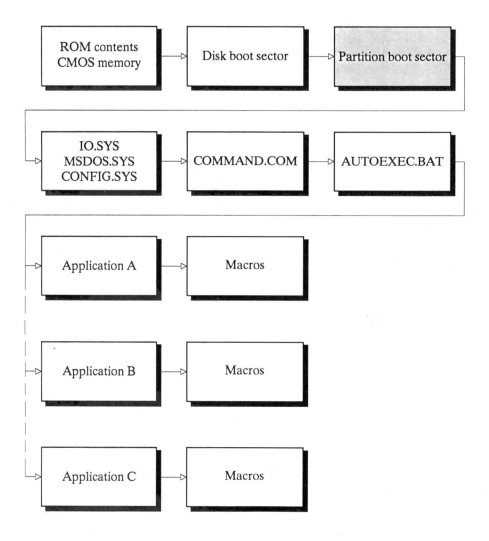

Fig. 2-1 Bootstrapping procedure

On a PC, the attack points are most easily listed by analysing the steps which are performed when the PC is started (bootstrapped), either by switching it on, or by performing a so-called 'warm boot' (pressing the Ctrl, Alt and Del keys simultaneously).

The bootstrapping procedure is shown in Fig. 2-1 and consists of the following steps:

1. When the computer is switched on, or a warm boot is performed (Ctrl-Alt-Del), a PC first executes the program held in its ROM (Read Only Memory). The ROM program tests the drives for the first one containing a disk, loads into memory the contents of the first sector on the disk (the Disk Bootstrap Sector), which is a short program, and starts executing it. If the disk does not contain a recognisable bootstrap sector, the computer displays the message 'Non-system disk', or similar, and waits for the user to insert a 'system' disk.

   On IBM-AT computers, the system will also access the CMOS memory prior to performing this step. Various system parameters in the CMOS memory can be set up (usually using the SETUP utility supplied with DOS).

2. On hard disks the disk bootstrap sector program reads in the partition bootstrap sector, which in turn reads in DOS and transfers control to it.

3. On floppy disks the bootstrap sector program reads the operating system (DOS) from disk into memory and transfers control to it.

4. DOS is contained in the first two files found in the directory which are usually called IO.SYS and MSDOS.SYS (or IBMBIO.SYS and IBMDOS.SYS), although different names are also used. DOS then accesses the file CONFIG.SYS which describes the desired configuration of the system (file buffer allocation, device drivers etc.). Device drivers like ANSI.SYS are loaded into memory at this stage.

5. DOS then loads COMMAND.COM and executes it. COMMAND.COM processes the commands entered by the user.

6. The AUTOEXEC.BAT file is then executed, thus completing the bootstrapping procedure. If no AUTOEXEC.BAT file is found, the system prompts the user for date and time.

7. The user is then presented with the system prompt and the system awaits user commands. Any command is either an internal DOS command, the name of an EXE file, the name of a COM file, or the name of a BAT file. The system will search for these files in all subdirectories specified in the PATH command and execute the first one it finds. Programs can also load executable overlay files (OVL) as and when needed. Overlay files have extensions such as OVL, OV1, OV2 etc.

8. Applications often use macros which are, in effect, executable code. This can take the form of interpreted BASIC commands, spreadsheet macros, word-processing macros and so on.

A virus must penetrate and change one or more of the above steps in order to execute. Let us consider each in turn, in terms of their vulnerability to attack by current viruses.

1. **Program held in ROM** - no chance of attack since ROM is not modifiable once programmed. The CMOS memory does not contain any executable code and cannot contain a virus.

2. **Disk boot sector and partition boot sector on hard disks** - at least one virus (*New Zealand*) attacks the disk boot sector, while several attack the partition boot sector (e.g. *Italian* and *Mistake*).

3. **Disk boot sector on floppy disks** - several viruses attack the disk boot sector.

4. **DOS files IO.SYS and MSDOS.SYS** - possible attack points, although to date no viruses have infected either file. CONFIG.SYS is a text file, and cannot contain a virus, but it could easily load and execute any virus written as a device driver.

5. **COMMAND.COM** - at least one virus (*Lehigh*) targets this file specifically.

6. **AUTOEXEC.BAT** - a possible attack point, though normally affected by Trojan horses rather than viruses.

7. **Applications EXE, COM and BAT files** - several viruses attack these files. Overlay files have not so far been subject to attack, although there is no reason why they should not be, other than that their precise structure is not standardised.

8. **Files with macros** - no viruses, other than experimental ones, have been shown to attack these files.

To keep the system free from viruses the user must make sure that the code executed during all of the above steps is virus-free and uncorrupted. Unfortunately, this is harder than it seems since viruses can infect a number of these steps and lay obstacles in front of the specialist trying to discover them.

2.3 VIRUS CARRIER MEDIA

Any medium which can be used for transmission of executables is a potential carrier of **parasitic viruses**. Any medium which can be used to bootstrap the PC can also be used to carry **bootstrap sector viruses**. For a description of these virus types see section 3.1: 'Virus Types According to the Point of Attack'.

The PC becomes infected with a **parasitic virus** when the user executes an infected program. The system becomes infected with a **bootstrap sector virus** when bootstrapped from an infected medium.

2.3.1 FLOPPY DISKS

Floppy disks are the most common medium for information exchange. They are used for distributing programs or exchanging information between PCs and can act as carriers of parasitic viruses which hide in any executable on the disk, or of bootstrap sector viruses, which hide in the bootstrap sector of the disk.

Executing an infected program need not be a conscious action on the part of the user. If the virus has infected COMMAND.COM (like the *Lehigh* virus), the system will become infected automatically if it is bootstrapped from an infected disk. This can happen quite easily if a floppy is left in a PC overnight, and switched on in the morning (I have certainly done this more than once). The PC can also become infected if a short power cut occurs while the machine is unattended with floppy disk left in the drive. When the user returns to the PC he will probably not notice that the PC has been bootstrapped in his absence.

Some users prevent bootstrapping from floppy disks in ATs and compatibles by setting the system configuration in the CMOS memory so that the computer "thinks" that it has no floppy disk drives. This forces the PC to bootstrap from its hard disk. Disabling the use of floppy disk drives also disables loading of any potentially dangerous disks. Various access control products provide a similar function for XTs, as does a small electronic circuit board from Uti-Maco Software (see appendix D for address) which fits between the floppy disk drive and data cable.

2.3.2 REMOVABLE HARD DISKS

Removable hard disks are becoming more popular in secure systems where the mass storage device has to be physically locked away when the PC is not attended. However, as they can be used on various PCs, they can act as carriers of both parasitic and bootstrap sector viruses.

2.3.3 MAGNETIC CARTRIDGES

Magnetic cartridges are normally used for storing PC backups. The PC cannot be booted from them, and as such, they can only carry parasitic viruses.

2.3.4 OTHER STORAGE MEDIA

There are several other storage media used with PCs (Bernoulli drives, optical disks, 1/2" magnetic tapes etc.). **As a rule, if the medium can be used to bootstrap the PC, it should be considerd capable of carying bootstrap sector viruses, as well as parasitic viruses. If the medium cannot be used to bootstrap the PC, it can only carry parasitic viruses.**

2.3.5 MODEMS

Modems offer the PC a means of communicating with other PCs, normally via an intermediate storage facility such as bulletin board or electronic mail servers. If these offer the facility to upload and download executable images, they can act as carriers of parasitic viruses. Bootstrap sector viruses cannot be transmitted unwittingly via modems.

2.4 VIRUS INFILTRATION ROUTES AND METHODS

Some user actions have been shown to carry a high risk of becoming infected with viruses. The following list of routes and methods of virus infiltration has been assembled by analysing real-life cases in which organisations and individuals became infected.

2.4.1 PIRATED SOFTWARE

It is easy to copy software and in most countries it is illegal to do so. But unless it is done on a large scale, the risk of prosecution at the moment is much smaller than the risk of contracting a virus infection. Games are probably the most commonly pirated software and they tend to move between PC users at a far greater speed than 'serious' pirated software. For this reason, they are also most prone to picking up a parasitic virus on the way.

2.4.2 BULLETIN BOARDS

Bulletin boards normally provide the means of downloading and uploading software which is classified either as 'public domain' (free for all) or 'shareware' (copy freely, but pay if you use it). Most reputable boards are run under the close supervision of the SYSOP, the SYStem OPerator, who is at great pains to ensure the integrity of the software available from the bulletin board.

However, unless the software is completely trivial, it is impossible to analyse it in full; it is normally easier to write an application from scratch than to analyse a compiled program. It is only marginally easier to test software for possible virus infection.

Bulletin board software is almost always distributed in compressed (*ARC* or *ZIP*) format which cannot be easily infected. This helps prevent infection unless the software is unpacked, (accidentally) infected and repacked at some stage.

2.4.3 SHAREWARE

Shareware is an attractive concept developed in the USA. The software carries the traditional copyright, but anybody is encouraged to copy it and pass it on to others. If anybody ends up using it, he is under moral obligation to send a small sum (usually

$20 to $50) to the author. The attraction lies in the fact that one ends up trying the software before paying for it. Market forces ensure the distribution and survival of good software and the eventual demise of rubbish. Unfortunately, in the age of viruses, shareware distribution is not without problems. Although most authors send 'the latest version' once payment has been received, one often ends up trying (and using) the original version obtained from a friend of a friend of a friend. By the time one gets 'the latest version', the computer may be infected many times over with any viruses the original software picked up on the way.

Some companies distribute shareware through catalogues, guaranteeing 'the latest version' when shareware is purchased. Obviously, this is better than the 'friend of a friend of a friend' method, and the company has a vested interest in distributing uncontaminated software. However, the problem remains of determining whether the software was contaminated at source with Trojan horses; the only person who may know the answer is the author.

Many shareware packages now include a checksum program and a list of correct checksums for all files supplied with the package. As long as the checksum program is not infected and the checksumming algorithm is cryptographically strong, this provides an assurance of file integrity (see section 7.1.1: 'Checksumming Software').

Shareware is nevertheless a cheap way of obtaining software, some of which is of excellent quality.

2.4.4 PUBLIC DOMAIN SOFTWARE

Unlike shareware, public domain software is completely free for anybody to use. Unfortunately, it suffers from the same distribution risks as shareware, with the added disadvantage that there is often nobody to supply 'the latest version'.

There are a number of notable exceptions to the above, such as the *Kermit* communications package, which is fully supported by Columbia University in New York, USA. Anybody can obtain the latest version for a fee to cover administration costs.

2.4.5 SHARED PCS (PC AT HOME)

A surprisingly large number of infections in business PCs occur through the use of home computers for company work. The companies concerned usually have sound anti-virus security measures in place, but still suffer virus attacks by overlooking this loophole.

In one case an executive's 14-year old son used his father's home PC to play games downloaded from bulletin boards (unbeknown to his father). The executive, having brought home a report to finish, unwittingly took an infected disk back to work the next morning and in turn, infected his office PCs with the *Italian* virus. His son was out of favour for some time, but the company learned a valuable lesson.

2.4.6 SERVICE ENGINEERS

Traditionally, service engineers have been a great source of the latest games, diagnostics and similar software. They can often be seen carrying more floppy disks than tools. Seeing five or ten customers a day, they are an effective propagation medium for any copyable software.

In one recent case a service engineer on a visit to a government organisation in England demonstrated an entertaining program called 'MUSHROOM'. Everyone wanted to run MUSHROOM. Unfortunately, that copy of MUSHROOM.COM had been infected with the *Cascade* virus, which in turn spread to many other programs on the affected PCs. The engineer eventually examined the original source of the program and discovered that it was not infected. The infection was picked up along the way, probably on one of the customers' computers.

A lot can be done to prevent viruses from infiltrating organisations through this route. All diagnostic disks used by service engineers should be write-protected, or, alternatively, the customer should have a set of his own write-protected disks. Service engineers should resist the temptation to distribute software, which is not only dangerous, but also often illegal.

At least one large computer company has expressly prohibited its service engineers from carrying any floppy disks. All disks used on the customers' PCs, including diagnostics, must be either already in possession by the user or come shrink-wrapped from the factory.

2.4.7 SHRINK-WRAPPED SOFTWARE

Shrink-wrapped software normally refers to commercial software packages which come in a shrink-wrapped sealed container - usually for legislative purposes rather than anti-virus measures. By breaking the seal, the user implicitly agrees to abide by the manufacturer's terms and conditions. There is also a good chance that the software has not been tampered with from the time it left the manufacturing plant.

There has been at least one case of shrink-wrapped software containing a virus (the software was for Apple Macintosh). The company discovered the problem, recalled all the packages which had just reached the dealers' shelves and thus managed to contain the problem. Stringent QA (Quality Assurance) procedures were also introduced to prevent a repeat occurrence.

Although there is always a chance that shrink-wrapped software will contain a virus, the probability is normally extremely small. The reasons for this are twofold: Companies marketing shrink-wrapped software have a large investment in their products and a lot to loose from bad publicity should the products prove to be virus carriers. They also have sufficient profit margins on more expensive packages to provide stringent QA procedures, which aim to ensure the integrity of the software leaving the factory. The development of such software may take longer than Joe

Bloggs working in a garage on his own, but the result is a traceable step-by-step process in a controlled environment. This is necessary for efficient anti-virus measures.

Buying quality has always meant spending a bit more, and the situation is no different in computer software.

2.4.8 VIRUSES AND PC NETWORKS

Although the IBM-PC set a single standard which has been widely followed, PC networks were developed by several vendors, and there are no standards comparable to the PC. Fortunately, there seem to be a few 'winners' emerging from the network jungle, so there is hope of some standardisation in the future.

Simple networks normally allow several users to access the central file server, which is treated as a big shared disk. Anybody can write to it and access any directory. Such systems offer no security in general, as well as no security against viruses. If a user's PC becomes infected with a parasitic virus and the user executes a program residing on the file server, the program on the file server will become contaminated. Any other user executing that program from then on will infect his PC (Fig. 2-2).

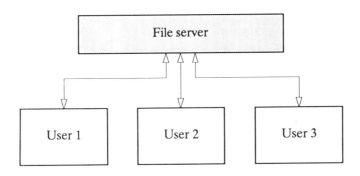

Fig. 2-2 Possible virus flow on simple unprotected networks

Few networks in use today are as primitive as that. Most offer some degree of protection against writing to designated areas, such as the directory containing executables. The best security features at present are offered by Novell *NetWare* which provides four different aspects of file-server security: the **login procedure**, **trustee rights**, **directory rights** and **file attributes**.

· The **login procedure** requires all users to identify themselves by a username and a password.

· **Trustee rights** are granted to each user by the 'network supervisor' and allow each user various actions like reading from files, writing to files, creating files, searching directories etc.

· **Directory rights** (read, write, open, close, delete) are set separately and can be used to limit the access to certain directories such as those containing executables.

· **File Attributes** (read-only, read-write, share) can be set separately.

The above security aspects mean that even if a user's PC becomes infected, the infection cannot spread to the file server (Fig. 2-3). This security **does** break down if the network supervisor's PC becomes infected though this is generally much less likely than an individual user's PC becoming infected.

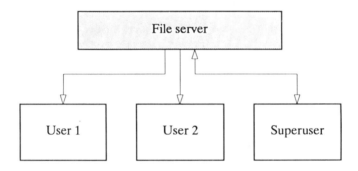

Fig. 2-3 Possible virus flow on protected networks

3

VIRUS STRUCTURE

It was truly a splendid structure,
and Yossarian throbbed with a mighty sense of accomplishment
each time he gazed at it and reflected that none of the work that had gone into it was
his.

J. Heller, Catch-22

A virus consists of two parts: **Self-replicating code** and the **'payload'**, which produces side-effects (Fig. 3-1). In a typical PC virus, the replicating code may have between 400 and 2000 bytes, while the size of the payload will depend on the side-effects. Typically this is a few hundred bytes.

Before infecting an executable, most viruses try to determine whether they have already infected it, by testing for some infection **signature**. If the signature (sometimes also referred to as "virus marker") is there, the executable is already infected and it will not be reinfected. The signature can have various forms. Some viruses use a sequence of characters like 'sURIV' (VIRUs spelled backwards) in a fixed position, others test the file size for divisibility by a number. At least one virus (*Jerusalem*) does not test correctly for its own signature, which results in reinfections and thus unlimited growth of executable images.

The side-effects of a virus are limited only by the imagination of the virus author and can range from annoyance to serious vandalism.

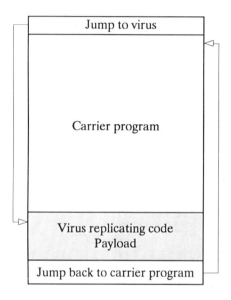

Fig. 3-1 Carrier program infected by a virus

3.1 VIRUS TYPES ACCORDING TO THE POINT OF ATTACK

Viruses can be divided into two categories according to the executable item which they infect: **Bootstrap sector viruses** and **Parasitic viruses**.

3.1.1 BOOTSTRAP SECTOR VIRUSES

Bootstrap sector viruses modify the contents of either the disk bootstrap sector or the partition bootstrap sector, depending on the virus and type of disk, usually replacing the legitimate contents with their own version. The original version of the modified sector is normally stored somewhere else on the disk, so that on bootstrapping, the virus version will be executed first. This normally loads the remainder of the virus code into memory, followed by the execution of the original version of the bootstrap sector (Fig. 3-2). From then on, the virus generally remains memory-resident until the computer is switched off. A bootstrap sector virus is thus able to monitor and interfere with the action of the operating system from the very moment it is loaded into memory.

The mechanism of a bootstrap sector virus normally uses three distinct components:

1. **the bootstrap sector** - replaced with a corrupted version; this is where the virus gains access.

2. **one previously unused sector** - for storing the original bootstrap sector.

3. **a number of previously unused sectors** - where the bulk of the virus code is stored.

Examples of bootstrap sector viruses include *Brain* (floppy disk bootstrap sector only), *Italian* (floppy disk bootstrap sector and hard disk partition bootstrap sector) and *New Zealand* (floppy disk and hard disk bootstrap sector).

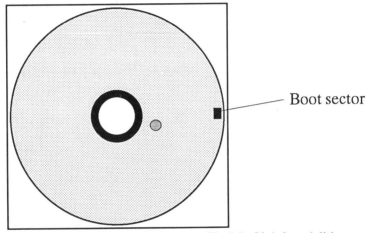

Fig. 3-2a Uninfected disk

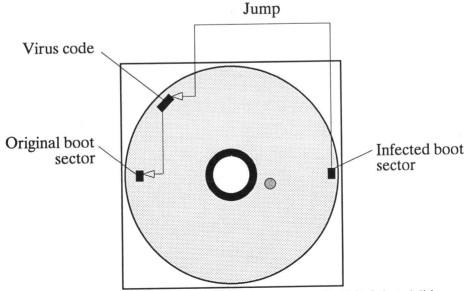

Fig. 3-2b Infected disk

3.1.2 PARASITIC VIRUSES

Parasitic viruses modify the contents of COM and/or EXE files. They insert themselves at the end or at the beginning of the file, leaving the bulk of the program intact (Fig. 3-3). The initial jump instruction in the program is modified, but program functionality is usually preserved. However there is at least one virus which overwrites the first few hundred bytes of the program, making it unusable.

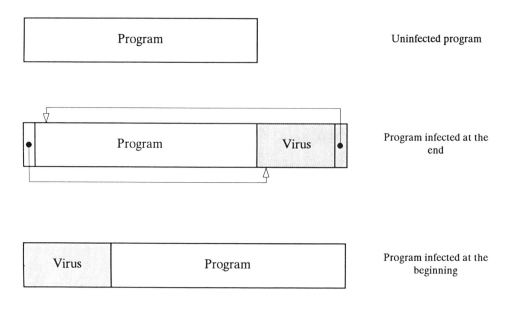

Fig. 3-3 Program infection with a parasitic virus

When an infected program is executed, the virus code is executed first. The virus then returns control to the original program, which executes normally. The extra execution time due to the virus is normally not perceptible to the user.

Most parasitic viruses, like *Cascade*, spread when another (uninfected) program is loaded and executed. Such a virus, being memory-resident, first inspects the program for infection already in place. If it is not infected, the virus will infect it. If it is already infected, further infection is not necessary (although some parasitic viruses like *Jerusalem* do reinfect ad infinitum). Infection by the *Cascade* virus is shown in Fig. 3-4.

Some viruses do not install themselves in memory, but spread by finding the first uninfected program on disk and infecting it. One such example is the *Vienna* virus.

```
C:\VIRUS>dir

 Volume in drive C has no label
 Directory of  C:\VIRUS

 .               <DIR>        8-01-88   12:01a
 ..              <DIR>        8-01-88   12:01a
 ALTER    COM      2725   12-26-83   12:51a
 WHEREIS  COM       640    9-03-86    3:48p
        4 File(s)   19636224 bytes free

C:\VIRUS>alter

You must specify a path.

C:>VIRUS>whereis

C:>VIRUS>dir

 Volume in drive C has no label
 Directory of  C:\VIRUS

 .               <DIR>        8-01-88   12:01a
 ..              <DIR>        8-01-88   12:01a
 ALTER    COM      2725   12-26-83   12:51a
 WHEREIS  COM      2341    9-03-86    3:48p
        4 File(s)   19634176 bytes free
```

Infect the PC by executing an infected application

Output from alter

Infect another COM file

Note size increase by 1701 bytes and no change of date / time

Fig. 3-4 Infecting an application with *Cascade*

3.2 VIRUS BEHAVIOUR AFTER INFECTION OF THE PC

3.2.1 MEMORY-RESIDENT VIRUSES

Memory-resident viruses install themselves into memory as Terminate and Stay Resident (TSR) processes when an infected program is executed. They will normally intercept one or more interrupts and infect other executables when certain conditions are fulfilled (e.g. when the user attempts to execute an application (*Cascade*) or when the user accesses a drive (*Brain*)). Switching the PC off will clear the virus from memory; warm bootstrapping with Ctrl-Alt-Del may not, as some viruses like *Yale* intercept the Ctrl-Alt-Del interrupt and survive the warm boot.

3.2.2 NON-MEMORY-RESIDENT VIRUSES

Non-memory-resident viruses are active only when an infected application is executed. They execute their code completely at that stage and do not remain in memory. Other executables are generally infected only when an infected program is executed (e.g. *Vienna* or *Datacrime*).

Although this approach may seem less infectious than one used by memory-resident viruses, the infectiousness of these viruses, in practice, is just as high, if not higher than that of the memory-resident viruses. They are also more difficult to spot, since they do not change the interrupt table or the amount of available memory, and their infectious behaviour can be more unpredictable.

3.2.3 HYBRIDS

Some viruses use a combination of these two methods. The *Typo* virus, for example, infects executables on invocation of an infected program, but also leaves a small TSR element in memory after infection. The TSR section contains the payload, while the non resident portion of the virus contains the replication code. In other hybrid viruses these functions might be allocated differently.

3.3 VIRUS HIDING MECHANISMS

Viruses use hiding mechanisms which allow them to replicate unnoticed, before delivering the 'payload'. This time delay before discovery is analogous to the incubation period in a biological disease, when the carrier of the disease is infectious, but does not exhibit any symptoms.

Current viruses employ two hiding mechanisms: Encryption (scrambling) and interrupt interception.

Carrier program	Virus
Program 1	DEYu*&81lp[@#
Program 2	DE132{+as$5\%6
Program 3	DE!"334%^dfs6456

Fig. 3-5 Three programs infected with an identical encrypted virus

3.3.1 ENCRYPTION

Encryption, or scrambling, of the virus code, is used by some viruses in order to make the majority of the virus code appear different in each infected application. This is designed to make the extraction of a fixed search pattern more difficult, since the majority of the virus code changes on every infection (Fig. 3-5). Before the virus code can be executed, it must be decrypted in order to become meaningful sequence of instructions. The decryption routine **must be in plain** (unencrypted) form and it usually contains about ten or twenty bytes which are identical and common to every infected executable (Shown as 'DE' in Fig. 3-5). The encryption key which most viruses use is linked to the length of the executable; an encrypted virus will look identical only when it uses the same encryption key to encrypt its code.

Although encryption algorithms in current viruses are simple and the keys are straight forward, the possibilities for introducing complications are practically endless. For example, the virus could use two stages of encryption, where the key for encrypting the second stage is stored in an encrypted form in the first stage. Alternatively, cryptographically stronger algorithms could be used in place of the simple functions like exclusive-or (XOR) in *Cascade*.

Such 'refinements' will make disassembly of the virus more difficult, but even the current encrypted viruses (which are comparatively simple) are not straight forward to disassemble. Encryption presents a further hurdle in the path of a virus researcher.

3.3.2 INTERRUPT INTERCEPTION

Interrupt interception can be used very successfully to hide the presence of a virus in an infected PC. PC-DOS applications use software interrupts to communicate with the operating system in a portable way. The jump addresses are stored in the

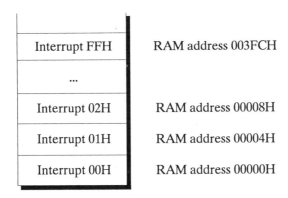

Interrupt FFH	RAM address 003FCH
...	
Interrupt 02H	RAM address 00008H
Interrupt 01H	RAM address 00004H
Interrupt 00H	RAM address 00000H

Each interrupt contains:
    Code Segment (CS) base address (16 bits)
    Instruction Pointer (IP) offset (16 bits)   Fig. 3-6 Interrupt table

interrupt table located at the beginning of memory (Fig. 3-6), so that when an application issues an interrupt, a jump occurs to a predetermined address. If a virus changes one or more of these addresses, any jumps to the operating system can be routed via the virus, which can then decide what to do with a particular request (Fig. 3-7). For example, if the *Brain* virus is active in memory and an application requests the operating system to read from disk the contents of sector 0 (the hiding place of *Brain*), the virus will return the contents of what the legitimate sector 0 would contain, instead of the actual contents. *Brain* achieves this by modifying ('hooking itself into') the interrupt table.

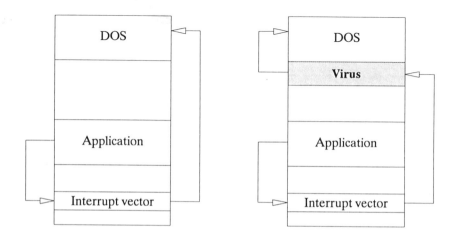

Fig. 3.7 Interrupt routing before and after infection

3.3.3 BINARY VIRUSES

Binary viruses are a special case of encrypted viruses. The principle is that a virus carries the replicating code in full, but only half of the payload. Only when the 'companion' virus is encountered (which carries the other half of the payload), the combination of the two payloads produces meaningful code which can be executed (Fig. 3-8). The combining could be done by performing an exclusive-or (XOR) operation on the two halves. In a binary virus, the payload cannot be analysed unless the researcher has access to both halves of the virus.

Although this concept has been sometimes quoted as a dangerous future development in virus sophistication, it has not been seen in any current viruses. The only virus which *may* have incorporated this concept is the *dBASE* virus. As part of the payload, the original virus contains the following sequence:

```
            CLI
            MOV     AX,3      ; Set count
LABEL:      MOV     CX,100H
            MOV     DX,0      ; Page 0 RAM
            MOV     DS,DX     ; Segment 0
            XOR     BX,BX     ; Offset 0
            PUSH    AX        ; Save the count
            INT     3H        ; ?
            INT     3H        ; ?
            POP     AX        ; Restore count
            INC     AX        ; Next
            CMP     AL,1AH    ; Reached 26 ?
            JL      LABEL     ; Go again
;           ...               ; Continue
```

This sequence does not do much *unless* either of the following happens:

1. A companion virus changes the two INT 3H instructions (which assemble as 1 byte each = 2 bytes) into one INT 26H instruction (which assembles as 2 bytes)

2. A companion virus changes the interrupt table so that the interrupt 3H points to interrupt 26H

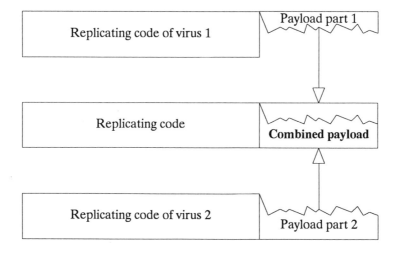

Fig. 3-8 Binary virus - two parts combining to get a meaningful payload

If either of the above happens, the payload becomes highly destructive. On triggering, the (modified) virus will overwrite the first 256 sectors of each drive from D: to Z: by using absolute disk write interrupt 26H.

Virus patterns for the *dBASE* virus shown in chapter 4 reflect the above possibility. The standard *dBASE* pattern is the one found in the seen and disassembled virus, while the *dBASE destroy* pattern is the pattern in the so far unseen (destructive) virus. Although this is one explanation for the *dBASE* mystery, other possibilities are that the seen version is the pre-release, non-destructive version, which could easily be modified into a destructive one, or, alternatively, a 'disarmed' version of the captured destructive virus.

3.4 VIRUS SIDE-EFFECTS

Virus side-effects (or the virus 'payload') are normally the first contact between the infected user and the virus. Not surprisingly, they are also the part which is most interesting for the majority of users.

They are normally the easiest part of the virus to program. They are also the easiest part to change. There have been several examples of mutated viruses which had their side-effects completely changed from the original (e.g. *Cascade-format* and *Cascade*).

Virus side-effects range from annoyance (such as the bouncing ball in the *Italian*), data modification (like the *dBASE* virus) to data destruction (*Datacrime* family). The side-effects are completely open to the imagination of the programmer.

When the first viruses appeared, their side-effects were on the whole confined to annoyance, which prompted several people to treat **all** viruses as innocuous, and as dangerous as a pet cat. Unfortunately, recent viruses are more like hungry tigers; fine behind bars in a zoo, but rather less so in the wild.

4

COMMON IBM-PC VIRUSES

You can be in the Horse Guards and still be common, dear.

Terence Rattigan, Separate Tables: "Table Number Seven"

4.1 VIRUS NAMES AND ALIASES

When a new virus is discovered by a researcher, the first problem is to establish whether the virus is a known one. Since that can take time, a researcher may decide on the name before announcing the find. The result of this is that multiple names for the same virus are common, and when a 'new' virus is reported, it is often only a known virus with a new name.

There is also a preference among some researchers to call parasitic viruses by a number, which is their infective length (the increase in the length of the infected executable). This can be very confusing since one virus can have several infective lengths (*Jerusalem* has an infective length of 1813 bytes for COM files and 1808 bytes for EXE files), and completely different viruses can have identical infective lengths (both *Agiplan* and *Zero Bug* have an infective length of 1536 bytes).

If you discover a new virus at some stage in the future, please do not rush to give it a name. First check whether the virus is already known and only if not, christen it with something suitable, which is preferably not its infective length. Names of viruses are normally related to virus side-effects (*Cascade*), strings embedded in the virus (*Suriv*) or the name chosen by the author and included in the virus (*Datacrime*).

4.2 VIRUS HEX PATTERNS

One common way of testing executable files for viruses is to search for recognition patterns known to be part of known viruses. These patterns are normally represented as hexadecimal digits and referred to as 'hex patterns'.

This section contains short descriptions and hexadecimal patterns of viruses seen by January 1990. This list is supplied by courtesy of the *Virus Bulletin* (see appendix A) and will invariably be out of date as soon as it is published. The reader is urged to treat it only as a sample of what viruses *could* be around and find most up-to-date information in one of the journals or bulletin boards listed in appendix A.

The hexadecimal (hex) patterns in the table are normally from 10 to 16 bytes long, and there is a very small, but finite, chance that one of these patterns will be found in some uninfected and innocuous executable. Data in executable images is not completely random, and certain sequences of instructions used in a virus can occur in a perfectly legitimate program. The pattern from a virus is normally chosen so as to be unlikely to occur in a legitimate program, **but there is a chance that this may happen**. For more information on extracting virus patterns see section 5.2: 'Dissection of a Captured Virus'.

If a pattern-checking program, such as SEARCH in appendix B, reports a pattern match, it does not necessarily mean that a virus has been found, but that a virus **may** have been found. However, before the problem is fully analysed, it is sensible to take anti-virus precautions as described in chapter 6: 'Anti-Virus Procedures'.

Each entry in the table consists of the virus group name in bold, its aliases and the virus type (see Fig. 4-1 for type codes). This is followed by a short description (if available) and a 10 to 16 byte hex pattern. Offset is the number of bytes from the virus entry point. For parasitic viruses the infective length (the amount by which the length of an infected file is increased) is also given.

Type codes:

C = Infects COM files
E = Infects EXE files
D = Infects DOS boot sector (Logical sector 0 on hard
    and floppy disks)
M = Infects disk boot sector (Absolute sector 0 on hard
    disk, Logical sector 0 on floppy)
N = Not memory-resident after infection
R = Memory-resident after infection

Fig. 4-1 Virus type codes

4.2.1 SEEN VIRUSES

405 - CN: Infects one COM file (on a different disk) each time an infected program is run by overwriting the first 405 bytes. If the length of the file is less than 405 bytes, it will be increased to 405. The virus only infects the current directory and does not recognise a file already infected.

```
405               26A2 4902 26A2 4B02 26A2 8B02 50B4 19CD      ; Offset 00A
```

Alabama - ER: Infective length is 1560 bytes.

```
Alabama           8CDD 33DB 8EDB 8B07 0B47 0274 7489 1F89      ; Offset 109
```

Brain, Ashar, Shoe - DR: Consists of a bootstrap sector and 3 clusters (6 sectors) marked as bad in the FAT. The first of these contains the original boot sector. In its original version it only infects 360K floppy disks and occupies 7K of RAM. It creates a label "(c) Brain" on an infected disk. There is a variation which creates a label "(c) ashar".

```
Brain             A006 7CA2 097C 8B0E 077C 890E 0A7C E857      ; Offset 158
```

Cascade, Fall, Russian - CR: This encrypted virus attaches itself to the end of a COM file, increasing its length by 1701 or 1704 bytes. The encryption key includes the length of the infected program, so infected files of different lengths will look different. After infection it becomes memory-resident and infects every COM file executed, including COMMAND.COM. The original version will produce a "falling characters" display if the system date is between 1st October and 31st December 1988. The formatting version will format the hard disk on any day between 1st October and 31st December of any year except 1993. Both activations occur a random time after infection with a maximum of 5 minutes.

```
Cascade (1) 01    0F8D B74D 01BC 8206 3134 3124 464C 75F8      ; Offset 012, 1701 bytes
                                                               ; Falling characters
Cascade (1) 04    0F8D B74D 01BC 8506 3134 3124 464C 75F8      ; Offset 012, 1704 bytes
                                                               ; Falling characters
Cascade (1) Y4    FA8B CDE8 0000 5B81 EB31 012E F687 2A01      ; Offset 000, 1704 bytes
                                                               ; Falling characters
Cascade format    0F8D B74D 01BC 8506 3134 3124 464C 77F8      ; Offset 012, 1704 bytes
                                                               ; Formats hard disk
```

Dark Avenger - CER: Appears to infect on file open and close as well as load and execute expanding the file by 1800 bytes. This means that a virus-scan program will cause it to infect every program on the disk. Only infects if program is at least 1775 bytes.

```
Dark Avenger      740E FA8B E681 C408 08FB                     ; Offset 068, 1800 bytes
```

Datacrime - CN: The virus attaches itself to the end of a COM file, increasing its length by 1168 or 1280 bytes. On execution of an infected program, the virus searches through full directory structure of drives C, D, A and B for an uninfected COM file which will be infected. Files with 7th letter D will be ignored (including

COMMAND.COM). If the date is on or after 13th October of any year, the first 9 tracks of the hard disk will be formatted. The format is low level after displaying the message:

```
DATACRIME VIRUS
RELEASED: 1 MARCH 1989
```

This message is stored in an encrypted form in the virus.

```
Datacrime (1)    3601 0183 EE03 8BC6 3D00 0075 03E9 0201    ; Offset 002, 1168 bytes

Datacrime (2)    3601 0183 EE03 8BC6 3D00 0075 03E9 FE00    ; Offset 002, 1280 bytes
```

Datacrime II - CEN: This encrypted virus attaches itself to the end of a COM or EXE file, increasing their length by 1514 bytes. The virus searches through the full directory structure of drives C, A and B for an uninfected COM or EXE file. It ignores any file if the second letter is B. If the date is on or after 13th October of any year, but not a Monday, a low level format of the first 9 tracks will be done on the hard disk after displaying the message:

```
DATACRIME II VIRUS
```

This message is stored in an encrypted form in the virus.

```
Datacrime II     2E8A 072E C605 2232 C2D0                   ; Offset 022, 1514 bytes
```

dBASE - CR: Transposes bytes in dBASE files (DBF). Creates the hidden file BUGS.DAT in the root directory of drive C: and generates errors if the absolute difference between the month of creation of BUGS.DAT and the current month is greater or equal to 3. Infective length is 1864 bytes. A disk-destroying version could be in the wild, but has not been seen.

```
dBASE            50B8 0AFB CD21 3DFB 0A74 02EB 8A56 E800    ; Offset 636, 1864 bytes

dBASE destroy    B900 01BA 0000 8EDA 33DB 50CD 2658 403C    ; Offset 735, 1864 bytes
```

Den Zuk, Search - DR: The majority of the virus is stored in a specially formatted track 40, head 0 sectors 33 to 41. When Ctrl-Alt-Del is pressed, the virus intercepts it and displays "DEN ZUK" sliding in from the sides of the screen. This does not happen if KEYBUK or KEYB is installed. Den Zuk will remove Brain and Ohio and replace them with copies of itself.

```
Den Zuk          FA8C C88E D88E D0BC 00F0 FBB8 787C 50C3    ; Offset 0
```

Disk Killer, Ogre - DR: The virus infects floppy and hard disks and if the computer is left on for more than 48 hours, it will encrypt the contents of the bootable disk partition. The infection of a disk occurrs by intercepting a disk read - INT 13H function 2. When the virus triggers, it displays the message "Disk Killer -- Version

1.00 by Ogre Software, 04/01/1989. Warning !! Don't turn off the power or remove the diskette while Disk Killer is Processing!".

```
Disk Killer      2EA1 1304 2D08 002E A313 04B1 06D3 E08E ; Offset 0C3
```

Fu Manchu - CER: The virus attaches itself to the beginning of a COM file or to the end of an EXE file. Infective length is 2086 bytes (COM) and 2080 (EXE). It is a rewritten version of the Jerusalem virus, but the marker is now "rEMHOr" and the preceding "sU" is now "sAX" (Sax Rohmer, creator of Fu Manchu). After installing itself as memory-resident, it will infect any COM or EXE file, except COMMAND.COM. EXE files are infected only once, unlike the original Jerusalem. One in sixteen times on infection a timer is installed, which will trigger a display "The world will hear from me again" after a random number of half-hours (max. 7.5 hours). The machine then reboots. The same message is also displayed on pressing Ctrl-Alt-Del, but the virus does not survive the reboot. If the date is after 1st August 1989, the virus monitors the keyboard buffer and adds derogatory comments to the names of politicians (Thatcher, Reagan, Botha and Waldheim), overstrikes two four-letter words, and displays "virus 3/10/88 - latest in the new fun line!" if "Fu Manchu" is typed. All messages are encrypted.

```
Fu Manchu        FCB4 E1CD 2180 FCE1 7316 80FC 0472 11B4   ; Offset 1EE
                                                           ; 2086 bytes COM files
                                                           ; 2080 bytes EXE files
```

Icelandic, Saratoga - ER: The virus attaches itself at the end of an EXE file and after becoming memory-resident, it will infect only one in ten (one in two for the Icelandic (2) variant) programs executed. When a program is infected, the disk is examined and if it has more than 20 MBytes, one cluster is marked as bad in the first copy of the FAT. There is a mutation which does not flag clusters. Version (1) will not infect the system unless INT 13H segment is 0700H or F000H, thus avoiding detection by anti-virus programs which hook into this interrupt. Version (3) does not flag clusters and bypasses all interrupt-checking programs.

```
Icelandic (1)    2EC6 0687 020A 9050 5351 5256 1E8B DA43   ; Offset 0C6, 656 bytes

Icelandic (2)    2EC6 0679 0202 9050 5351 5256 1E8B DA43   ; Offset 0B8, 642 bytes

Icelandic (3)    2EC6 066F 020A 9050 5351                  ; Offset 106, 632 bytes
```

Italian, Pingpong, Turin, Bouncing Ball, Vera Cruz - DR: The virus consists of a boot sector and one cluster (2 sectors) marked as bad in the first copy of the FAT. The first sector contains the rest of the virus while the second contains the original boot sector. It infects all disks which have at least two sectors per cluster and occupies 2K of RAM. It displays a single character "bouncing ball" if there is a disk access during the one-second interval in any multiple of 30 minutes on the system clock. The original version will hang when run on an 80286 or 80386 machine, but a new version has been reported which runs normally. If a warm boot is performed after the machine hangs, an uninfected disk will still become infected.

```
Italian-Gen      B106 D3E0 2DC0 078E C0BE 007C 8BFE B900   ; Offset 030

Italian          32E4 CD1A F6C6 7F75 0AF6 C2F0 7505 52E8   ; Offset 0F0
```

Jerusalem, PLO, Friday the 13th, Israeli - CER: The virus attaches itself to the beginning of a COM file or at the end of an EXE file. When an infected file is executed, the virus becomes memory-resident and will infect any COM or EXE program run, except COMMAND.COM. COM files are infected only once, while EXE files are re-infected every time that they are run. Infective length is 1813 bytes (COM) and 1808 bytes (EXE). The virus finds the end of EXE files from the information in the file header, and if this is less than the actual file length, the virus will overwrite part of the file. After the system has been infected for 30 minutes, row 5 column 5 to row 16 column 16 on the screen are scrolled up two lines, creating a "black window". The system then slows down, due to a time-wasting loop installed on each timer interrupt. If the system is infected when the date is set to 13th of any month which is also a Friday, every program run will be deleted.

```
Jerusalem         03F7 2E8B 8D11 00CD 218C C805 1000 8ED0      ; Offset 0AC
                                                               ; 1813 bytes COM files
                                                               ; 1808 bytes EXE files
```

Lehigh - CR: The virus only infects COMMAND.COM. It is 555 bytes long and becomes memory-resident when the infected copy is run. If a disk is accessed which contains an uninfected COMMAND.COM, the copy is infected. A count of infection generation is kept inside the virus, and when it reaches 4 (or 10 in a mutated version), the current disk is trashed each time a disk is infected, provided that (a) the current disk is either in the A drive or B drive, (b) the disk just infected is either the A drive or B drive and (c) the disk just infected is not the current one. The trashing is done by overwriting the first 32 sectors following the boot sector. Infection changes the date and time of infected COMMAND.COM.

```
Lehigh            8B54 FC8B 44FE 8ED8 B844 25CD 2106 1F33      ; Offset 1EF
```

Mistake - DR: Exchanges letters for phonetically similar ones (for example "C" & "K") while they are being output to the printer. Reportedly written in Israel. Almost certainly a mutation of the Italian virus.

```
Mistake           32E4 CD1A 80FE 0376 0A90 9090 9090 52E8      ; Offset 0F0
```

MIX1 - ER: The virus infects only EXE files attaching itself to the end. When an infected program is run, the virus will copy itself to the top of the free memory. Some programs may overwrite this area, causing the machine to crash. The virus traps printer and asynch interrupts and corrupts traffic by substituting characters. 50 minutes after infection, the virus alters Num Lock and Caps Lock keyboard settings. 60 minutes after infection, a display similar to the Italian virus (bouncing ball) will be produced. The virus will infect every tenth program run. Infected files always end in "MIX1" and the infective length of MIX1 is 1618 to 1633 bytes and MIX1-2 1636-1651 bytes.

```
MIX1              B800 008E C026 803E 3C03 7775 095F 5E59      ; Offset 02E

MIX1-2            B800 008E C0BE 7103 268B 3E84 0083 C70A      ; Offset 02A
```

New Zealand, Stoned, Marijuana - MR: The virus consists of a boot sector only. It infects all disks and occupies 2K of RAM. On floppy disks, the sector 0 is infected, while on the hard disks the physical sector 0 (Master boot sector) is infected. The original boot sector is stored in track 0 head 1 sector 3 on a floppy disk and track 0 head 0 sector 2 on a hard disk. The boot sector contains two character strings: "Your PC is now Stoned!" and "LEGALISE MARIJUANA" but only the former one is displayed once in eight times, and only if booted from floppy disk. The version (2) stores the original boot sector at track 0 head 0 sector 7 on a hard disk. The second string is not transferred when a hard disk is infected. A mutation has been reported in Australia which also displays "LEGALISE MARIJUANA".

```
New Zealand (1)    0400 B801 020E 07BB 0002 B901 0033 D29C    ; Offset 043

New Zealand (2)    0400 B801 020E 07BB 0002 33C9 8BD1 419C    ; Offset 041
```

Pentagon - DR: The virus consists of a boot sector and two files. The sample obtained does not work, but it contains the code which would survive a warm boot (Ctrl-Alt-Del). It could only infect 360K floppy disks, and will look for and remove Brain from any disk it infects. It occupies 5K of RAM.

```
Pentagon           8CC8 8ED0 BC00 F08E D8FB BD44 7C81 7606    ; Offset 037
```

South African, Friday the 13th, Miami, Munich, Virus-B - CN: Infective length is 419 bytes, but some reports suggest between 415 and 544 bytes. Does not infect files with Read-Only flag set. Virus-B is a non-destructive mutation containing South African 2 pattern. COMMAND.COM is not infected. Every file run on a Friday 13th will be deleted.

```
South African 1    1E8B ECC7 4610 0001 E800 0058 2DD7 00B1    ; Offset 158

South African 2    1E8B ECC7 4610 0001 E800 0058 2D63 00B1    ; Offset 158
```

Spanish, 2930 - CER: Earlier version of Traceback. There is a version which extends files by 3031 bytes.

```
Spanish            E829 06E8 E005 B419 CD21 8884 E300 E8CE    ; Offset ?
```

Suriv 1.01, April 1st COM - CR: A precursor to Jerusalem infecting only COM files with the virus positioned at the beginning of the file. Infective length is 897 bytes. If the date is 1st April, the virus will display "APRIL 1ST HA HA HA YOU HAVE A VIRUS" and the machine will lock. If the date is after 1st April 1988, the virus produces the message "YOU HAVE A VIRUS !!!" but the machine will not lock. The virus is memory-resident and will not infect COMMAND.COM.

```
Suriv 1.01         0E1F B42A CD21 81F9 C407 721B 81FA 0104    ; Offset 304, 897 bytes
```

Suriv 2.01, April 1st EXE - ER: A precursor to Jerusalem infecting only EXE files with the virus positioned at the beginning of the file. Infective length is 1488 bytes. If the date is 1st April, the virus will display "APRIL 1ST HA HA HA YOU HAVE

A VIRUS". If the year is 1980 (DOS default) or the day is Wednesday after 1st April 1988, the machine will lock one hour after infection.

```
Suriv 2.01       81F9 C407 7228 81FA 0104 7222 3C03 751E      ; Offset 05E, 1488 bytes
```

Suriv 3.00, Israeli - CER: An earlier version of Jerusalem infecting COM and EXE files and displaying the side-effects 30 seconds after infection instead of 30 minutes. Infective length is 1813 bytes (COM) and 1808 bytes (EXE). Program delete does not work.

```
Suriv 3.00       03F7 2E8B 8D15 00CD 218C C805 1000 8ED0      ; Offset 0B0
                                                              ; 1813 COM files
                                                              ; 1808 EXE files
```

Syslock - CEN: This encrypted virus attaches itself to the end of a COM or an EXE file. Infective length is 3551 bytes. It infects a program one in four times when executed. Will not infect if environment contains SYSLOCK=@.

```
Syslock          8AE1 8AC1 3306 1400 3104 4646 E2F2 5E59      ; Offset 0, 3551 bytes
```

Traceback - CER: This virus attaches itself to the end of a COM or an EXE file. Infective length is 3066 bytes. It becomes memory-resident when the first infected program is run and will infect any program run. If the date is 5th December or later, the virus will look for and infect one COM or EXE file either in the current directory or the first one found starting with the root directory. If the date is 28th December 1988 or later, the virus produces a display similar to Cascade one hour after infection. If nothing is typed, the screen restores itself after one minute. Display will repeat every hour.

```
Traceback        B419 CD21 89B4 5101 8184 5101 8408 8C8C      ; Offset 104, 3066 bytes
```

Typo, Typo COM, Fumble - CR: Infects all COM files in the subdirectory on odd-numbered days of every month. If typing fast, substitutes keys with the ones adjacent on the keyboard. Infective length is 867 bytes.

```
Typo             5351 521E 0656 0E1F E800 005E 83EE 24FF ; Offset 01D, 867 bytes
```

Vienna, Austrian, Unesco, DOS62, Lisbon - CN: The virus infects the end of COM files. Infective length is 648 bytes. It looks through the current directory and the directories in the PATH for an uninfected COM file. One file in eight becomes overwritten. Seconds stamp of an infected file is set to 62.

```
Vienna (1)       8BF2 83C6 0A90 BF00 01B9                     ; Offset 005, 648 bytes

Vienna (2)       FC8B F281 C60A 00BF 0001 B903 00F3 A48B      ; Offset 004, 648 bytes

Vienna (3)       FC89 D683 C60A 90BF 0001 B903 00F3 A489      ; Offset 004
```

Virus-90 - CN: The author of this virus uploaded the virus to a number of Bulletin Boards, stating that the source was available for $20. When an infected program is run it will display the message "Infected", infect a COM file in drive A: and display the message "Done". Infective length is 857 bytes.

```
Virus-90          558B 2E01 0181 C503 0133 C033 BBB9 0900      ; Offset 01E
```

Yale, Alameda, Merritt - DR: This virus consists of a boot sector and infects floppies in A drive only. It becomes memory-resident and occupies 1K of RAM. The original boot sector is held in track 39 head 0 sector 8. The machine will hang if the virus is run on an 80286 or 80386 machine. If a warm boot is performed after the machine hangs, an uninfected disk will still become infected. It has been assembled using A86 and contains code to format track 39 head 0, but this is not accessed. Survives a warm boot.

```
Yale              BB40 008E DBA1 1300 F7E3 2DE0 078E C00E      ; Offset 009
```

Yankee - CER: Infective length 2885 bytes.

```
Yankee            E800 005B 81EB D407 2EC6 875C 00FF FC2E      ; Offset 0
```

Zero Bug, Palette - CR: Infective length is 1536, attaches itself to the beginning of COM file. The virus modifies the number of seconds to 62 (like Vienna). If the virus is active in memory and the DIR command is issued, the file length of infected files will be identical to that before the infection. A mutation called Palette (infective length 1538 bytes) has also been reported.

```
Zero Bug          81C9 1F00 CD21 B43E CD21 5A1F 59B4 43B0      ; Offset 100
Palette           EB2B 905A 45CD 602E C606 2506 0190 2E80      ; Offset ?, 1538 bytes
```

4.2.2 REPORTED VIRUSES

4K, IDF, Israeli Defence Forces - CER: Infective length is 4096 bytes.

```
4K                E808 0BE8 D00A E89A 0AE8 F60A E8B4 0A53      ; Offset 239
```

Agiplan - CR: Infective length is 1536, attaches itself to the beginning of a COM file.

```
Agiplan           E9CC 0390 9090 9090 9C50 31C0 2E38 26DA      ; Offset 0 (?)
```

AIDS: Not to be confused with the AIDS Trojan, this virus overwrites COM files and is about 12K long.

Amstrad - CN: Adds 847 bytes to the front of any COM file in the current directory. The virus is only 334 bytes long, which makes it the shortest PC virus known. The rest contains the text advertising Amstrad computers.

```
Amstrad           C706 0E01 0000 2E8C 0610 012E FF2E 0E01      ; Offset 114
```

Century A: As Jerusalem-C, but activation date is 1st January 2000. Destroys FAT.

Century B: As Jerusalem-C, but produces a wait during the execution of BACKUP.COM

Chaos: A new and changed mutation of Brain

December 24th - ER: A mutation of the Icelandic (3) virus. It will infect one out of every 10 EXE files run, which grow by 848-863 bytes. If an infected file is run on December 24th, it will stop any other program from running and display the message "Gledileg jol" ("Merry Christmas" in Icelandic).

```
December 24th      C606 7E03 FEB4 5290 CD21 2E8C 0645 0326      ; Offset 044
```

Do-nothing - R

GhostBalls - CN: A strain of Vienna virus. Seconds field changed to 62, as in Vienna. Infective length is 2351 bytes and the virus attaches itself to the end of the file. When run, it will infect other COM files and try to place a modified copy of the Italian virus into boot sector of drive A:. This copy of the Italian runs on 286 machines but is non-infective. Virus contains text "GhostBalls, Product of Iceland".

```
GhostBalls         AE75 EDE2 FA5E 0789 BC16 008B FE81 C71F      ; Offset 051
```

Jerusalem-A: does not display black-hole in the screen

Jerusalem-B: EXE re-infection bug removed

Jerusalem-C: no slow-down effect

Jerusalem-D: destroys FAT in 1990

Jerusalem-E: destroys FAT in 1992

MachoSoft - CEN: Swaps every string "MicroSoft" with "MachoSoft" on the hard disk. Searches 20 sectors at a time, storing the last sector searched in IBMNETIO.SYS which is marked hidden and system. After searching the last sector it starts again. This will only happen after 1st January 1985 and if the environment variable VIRUS is not set to OFF. Infective length is 3550 to 3560 bytes. Random directory search for uninfected files. Infects COMMAND.COM.

```
MachoSoft          5051 56BE 5900 B926 0890 D1E9 8AE1 8AC1      ; Offset ?
```

Missouri - D

Nichols - D

Ohio - DR: Boot sector virus, probably an older version of Den Zuk

Oropax, Music virus - CR: Infected files increase by between 2756 & 2806 bytes. Total length becomes divisible by 51. 5 minutes after the infection, the virus plays three different tunes with a 7-minute interval. Does not infect COMMAND.COM.

```
Oropax          06B8 E033 CD21 3CFF 7423 8CCE 8EC6 8B36
```

Perfume - CR: The infected program will sometimes ask the user a question and not run unless the answer is 4711 (name of a perfume). The virus will look for COMMAND.COM and infect it. Infective length is 765 bytes.

```
Perfume         FCBF 0000 F3A4 81EC 0004 06BF BA00 57CB    ; Offset 0AA
```

Screen - CR: Infects all COM files in current directory, including any already infected, before going resident. Every few minutes it transposes two digits in any block of four on the screen.

Sunday - CER: Variation of Jerusalem. Infective length is 1631 bytes (EXE) and 1636 (COM). Activates on Sunday and displays message "Today is SunDay! Why do you work so hard? All work and no play make you a dull boy."

Swap - DR: Does not infect until ten minutes after boot. One bad cluster on track 39, sectors 6 & 7 (head unspecified). Uses 2K of RAM. Infects floppy disks only. Does not store the original boot sector anywhere. Virus creates a display similar to Cascade, but is transmitted via boot sector.

```
Swap            31C0 CD13 B802 02B9 0627 BA00 01BB 0020    ; Offset ?
```

Sylvia - CN: The virus displays the message "This program is infected by a HARMLESS Text-Virus V2.1", "Send a FUNNY postcard to: Sylvia Verkade, Duinzoom 36b, 3235 CD Rockanje, The Netherlands", "You might get an ANTIVIRUS program....." when an infected program is executed, but if the above text is tampered with, the (encrypted) message "F*** YOU LAMER !!!!", "system halted....$" will be displayed. When an infected program is run, the virus will look for 5 COM files on drive C: and the current drive. COMMAND.COM, IBMBIO.COM and IBMDOS.COM are not infected. The virus adds 1301 bytes to the beginning of the infected files and 31 bytes at the end.

```
Sylvia          CD21 EBFE C3A1 7002 A378 0233 C0A3 9E02    ; Offset 229
```

Vacsina - CER: Infective length 1206 to 1221 bytes (COM) and 1338 to 1353 bytes (EXE). After a successful infection of a COM file, a bell is sounded. Infects any file loaded via INT 21 function 4B (load and execute), i.e. COM, EXE, OVL and APP (GEM) files. Checks version number of itself (current is 5) and replaces with newer code.

Vcomm - ER: When an infected program is run, it will infect one EXE file in the current directory. Infected programs are padded so that their length becomes a multiple of 512 bytes. The virus then adds 537 bytes to the length of the file, as well as installing a memory-resident part which intercepts any disk-write and changes it into a disk-read.

W13 - CN: Fairly primitive viruses in two mutations: 534 bytes and 507 bytes long. The second version has some bugs corrected.

4.2.3 AIDS TROJAN HORSE

AIDS disk: Widely distributed disk which is an extortion attempt. Installs multiple hidden directories and files, as well as AIDS.EXE in the main directory and REM$.EXE in a hidden subdirectory ($ is the non-printing character FF Hexadecimal).

```
REM$.EXE          4D5A 0C01 1E01 0515 6005 0D03 FFFF 3D21      ; Offset 0

AIDS.EXE          4D5A 1200 5201 411B E006 780C FFFF 992F      ; Offset 0
```

5

WHERE DO VIRUSES COME FROM ?

*Ever since Sherlock Holmes most Englishmen have been born
with a detective novel attached to their umbilical cords.*

Tristram Busch, Secret Service Unmasked

5.1 WHO WRITES VIRUSES AND WHY ?

It is not easy to establish the origins of viruses, since it is rare to find any firm clues in the virus code. One notable exception is the *Brain* virus which has a name, address and telephone number embedded in the bootstrap sector (Fig. 5-1). *Brain* was written by two computer shop owners in Pakistan.

Some viruses have been traced back to their sources by comparing various versions and 'improvements' which authors (or infected users) may have made to the virus. This is how the *Italian* virus was traced back to the Polytechnic of Turin and the *Jerusalem* virus to the Hebrew University in Jerusalem.

A number of groups have been identified as potential (high likelihood) originators of viruses. It is also interesting to analyse their motivation from the psychiatric point of view.

5.1.1 HACKERS

Hackers are people analogous to drug addicts. They need their 'fix' and cannot leave the machine alone. Like addicts they seek novelty and new experiences. Writing a

```
000000    fa e9 4a 01 34 12 00 05    08 00 01 00 00 00 00 20    ..J.4... .......
000010    20 20 20 20 20 20 57 65    6c 63 6f 6d 65 20 74 6f           We lcome to
000020    20 74 68 65 20 44 75 6e    67 65 6f 6e 20 20 20 20    the Dun geon
000030    20 20 20 20 20 20 20 20    20 20 20 20 20 20 20 20
000040    20 20 20 20 20 20 20 20    20 20 20 20 20 20 20 20
000050    20 28 63 29 20 31 39 38    36 20 42 61 73 69 74 20    (c) 198 6 Basit
000060    26 20 41 6d 6a 61 64 20    28 70 76 74 29 20 4c 74    & Amjad (pvt) Lt
000070    64 2e 20 20 20 20 20 20    20 20 20 20 20 20 20 20    d.
000080    20 42 52 41 49 4e 20 43    4f 4d 50 55 54 45 52 20    BRAIN C OMPUTER
000090    53 45 52 56 49 43 45 53    2e 2e 37 33 30 20 4e 49    SERVICES ..730 NI
0000a0    5a 41 4d 20 42 4c 4f 43    4b 20 41 4c 4c 41 4d 41    ZAM BLOC K ALLAMA
0000b0    20 49 51 42 41 4c 20 54    4f 57 4e 20 20 20 20 20    IQBAL T OWN
0000c0    20 20 20 20 20 20 20 20    20 20 20 4c 41 48 4f 52            LAHOR
0000d0    45 2d 50 41 4b 49 53 54    41 4e 2e 2e 50 48 4f 4e    E-PAKIST AN..PHON
0000e0    45 20 3a 34 33 30 37 39    31 2c 34 34 33 32 34 38    E :43079 1,443248
0000f0    2c 32 38 30 35 33 30 2e    20 20 20 20 20 20 20 20    ,280530.
000100    20 20 42 65 77 61 72 65    20 6f 66 20 74 68 69 73      Beware  of this
000110    20 56 49 52 55 53 2e 2e    2e 2e 2e 43 6f 6e 74 61     VIRUS.. ...Conta
000120    63 74 20 75 73 20 66 6f    72 20 76 61 63 63 69 6e    ct us fo r vaccin
000130    61 74 69 6f 6e 2e 2e 2e    2e 2e 2e 2e 2e 2e 2e 2e    ation... ........
000140    2e 2e 2e 2e 20 24 23 40    25 24 40 21 21 20 8c c8    .... $#@ %$@!! ..
000150    8e d8 8e d0 bc 00 f0 fb    a0 06 7c a2 09 7c 8b 0e    ........ ..|..|..
000160    07 7c 89 0e 0a 7c e8 57    00 b9 05 00 bb 00 7e e8    .|...|.W ......~.
000170    2a 00 e8 4b 00 81 c3 00    02 e2 f4 a1 13 04 2d 07    *..K.... ......-.
000180    00 a3 13 04 b1 06 d3 e0    8e c0 be 00 7c bf 00 00    ........ ....|...
000190    b9 04 10 fc f3 a4 06 b8    00 02 50 cb 51 53 b9 04    ........ ..P.QS..
0001a0    00 51 8a 36 09 7c b2 00    8b 0e 0a 7c b8 01 02 cd    .Q.6.|.. ...|....
0001b0    13 73 09 b4 00 cd 13 59    e2 e7 cd 18 59 5b 59 c3    .s.....Y ....Y[Y.
0001c0    a0 0a 7c fe c0 a2 0a 7c    3c 0a 75 1a c6 06 0a 7c    ..|....| <.u....|
0001d0    01 a0 09 7c fe c0 a2 09    7c 3c 02 75 09 c6 06 09    ...|.... |<.u....
0001e0    7c 00 fe 06 0b 7c c3 00    00 00 00 32 e3 23 4d 59    |....|.. ...2.#MY
0001f0    f4 a1 82 bc c3 12 00 7e    12 cd 21 a2 3c 5f 0c 05    .......~ ..!.<_..
```

Fig. 5-1 *Brain* virus bootstrap sector

virus gives them this, but unlike addicts who get immediate relief after a fix, they are not usually present when the virus triggers and releases the payload.

5.1.2 FREAKS

This is an irresponsible subgroup of hackers, in the same way that some drug addicts remain reasonably responsible, while others (psychopaths) become irresponsible. They have serious social adjustment problems and often have a general, unspecified grudge against society. They have no sense of responsibility or remorse about what they do, and are prepared to exploit others in order to achieve their aims.

There are several reasons why freaks write viruses: Some do it for 'fun', others for money. Some of them may be mentally distressed, sick of their life or family and want to 'hit out'. There is some analogy between freak virus writers and the poisoner who delivers his potion, leaves and is untraced, and in his absence the victim falls.

They may sometimes include 'a message' in the virus ("Your PC is now Stoned!" and "LEGALISE MARIJUANA" in the *New Zealand* virus) and there may be some overlaps between freaks and terrorists who are motivated politically.

5.1.3 UNIVERSITY STUDENTS

Most universities offer free, often uncontrolled, computer facilities to students. Illegal software copying is widespread, and it is not accidental that there have been a number of virus outbreaks in academic environments, not necessarily caused by 'in-house' viruses. The technical ability necessary to write a virus is within the reach of a first-year computer science student, who may see such a project as an intellectual challenge.

This group is not only a potential source of PC viruses, but also a potential source of mainframe viruses. Whereas average members of the public can buy a cheap PC comparatively easily, they cannot (yet) buy an IBM System 370 or a DEC VAX. Most students have access to mainframes, and it seems that it is likely to be only a matter of time before mainframe viruses emerge from academia.

5.1.4 EMPLOYEES

Companies normally perceive disgruntled employees as a major security risk, and it is possible that in the future virus attacks will come from that source. Although a computer-literate employee could write a virus from scratch, it is more likely that he would either implant an existing virus into his organisation's PCs or use a mutated virus as a weapon.

Readiness to cause damage by programming has already been shown by numerous cases of logic bombs placed by disgruntled employees into computer systems.

The motive for an employee writing and/or implanting a virus is often vindictiveness. There is, however, not a great deal of difference between revenge and extortion. The disgruntled employee may harbour a genuine grievance. The extortionist's desire for revenge is deeper (possibly subconscious) and he himself may not understand it. Vindictiveness may accompany a strong sense of morality or moral duty making a disgruntled employee, in some peoples' eyes (above all his own), a freedom fighter (cf. 'Terrorist Organisations').

5.1.5 COMPUTER CLUBS

Some computer clubs have been very active in providing their members with information on how to write viruses. For example the *Chaos Computer Club* (CCC) in Hamburg, West Germany, have produced a 'Virus Construction Set' for the Atari ST, which allows the construction of customised viruses and a selection of virus effects from a menu.

Other clubs have a history of creating viruses. The *Swiss Crackers Association* (SCA), for example, released a virus for the Amiga which displays

```
Something wonderful has happened. Your Amiga is alive...
```

Members of clubs usually have shared values and ideals. It is quite probable that real troublemakers will not join computer clubs; clubs are for the insecure, who gain a sense of security thorugh sharing.

5.1.6 TERRORIST ORGANISATIONS

Evidence that terrorist organisations are involved in virus-writing is scarce. The Italian Red Brigade's manifesto specifically includes destruction of computer systems as an objective, which could be done by means other than the traditional use of explosives.

The *Jerusalem* virus was reputedly written by sympathisers of the PLO, but several authoritative researchers have disputed this. The only evidence linking the virus with the PLO is the trigger date (Friday 13th), which coincided with the last day of the existence of the Palestinian state.

Terrorists are fanatics, for whom nothing else matters. They may have been indoctrinated from an early age and are loyal to a group which holds them (in return) in very high regard. They are, in their own eyes, modern-day martyrs.

5.2 DISSECTION OF A CAPTURED VIRUS

Once a virus has been discovered, a user's first instinct is often to eradicate all occurrences of it. However, one should always endeavour to 'capture' a virus sample for analysis, as this can be helpful to other sites infected with the same virus.

Even if the virus is not completely analysed immediately, a hexadecimal pattern can be extracted in a comparatively short time, which helps to detect occurrences of the same virus elsewhere.

The full analysis of a virus will invariably involve its full disassembly, i.e. reverse engineering its binary code into commented source code.

5.2.1 VIRUS DISASSEMBLY

Virus disassembly can be simplified by a number of commercially available disassemblers such as SOURCER (V Communications), but much can be done using DEBUG, a powerful tool supplied as a part of MS-DOS. DEBUG is comparatively simple to use and has a number of functions which make it suitable for the job. It can read disk sectors and files, disassemble areas of memory as well as single-step through a program.

Disassembling a virus is an iterative process which includes discovering first which parts of the virus are data areas (which are not going to be disassembled) and which are instructions. Once that has been done, the output of DEBUG can be redirected to a file which will contain the disassembled virus. Take as an example a hypothetical virus in the file VIR.COM, which has been analysed with DEBUG and which has a JMP 110H instruction as the first 3 bytes, followed by 13 bytes of data, followed by code from 110H to 432H. It is useful to build up the sequence of DEBUG commands in a file, to avoid re-typing them continuously. The file INSTR could contain the following DEBUG instructions:

```
U 100 102 ; Disassemble locations 100 to 102
D 103 10F ; Dump locations 103 10F
U 110 432 ; Disassemble locations 110 to 432
Q ; Quit
```

DEBUG would then be invoked with the command

```
DEBUG VIR.COM <INSTR >VIR.ASM
```

which instructs it to read input from the file INSTR and output to file VIR.ASM which will contain the disassembly of VIR.COM.

U 100 102 will disassemble the first 3 bytes, D 103 10F will 'dump' 13 bytes of data in hexadecimal, while U 110 432 will disassemble instructions between addresses 110 and 432 Hex.

Disassembly of boot sector viruses can be slightly more complicated, as they normally occupy more sectors than just the boot sector. One has to analyse the boot sector first in order to discover which other sectors the virus uses. The principle of redirecting DEBUG input and output can be used in the same way as for parasitic viruses.

If a virus uses disk areas not accessible by DEBUG (for example the hard disk bootstrap sector in *New Zealand*), the best approach is to write a small assembly language program (using DEBUG) to issue the appropriate BIOS interrupt(s) and read in the disk area in question. This can be written out to a file (using DEBUG again), or analysed directly.

The program shown in Fig. 5-2 entered into DEBUG with the A (Assemble) command starting at location 100 will read the hard disk boot sector into memory by using the BIOS interrupt 13H, service 02. This service requires that ES:BX points to the memory location where the contents of the sector will be stored (in this example ES is set to the same value as DS) and BX is set to 800H in the current data segment.

Type G 10E which will execute the program, placing the breakpoint at location 10E (JMP 10E). Location DS:0800 can now be either Dumped or Unassembled (D 0800 or U 0800).

```
MOV AX,DS
MOV ES,AX ; Set ES
MOV AX,0201 ; Service 02H, 1 sector
MOV CX,0001 ; Track 0, sector 1
MOV DX,0080 ; Head 0, drive 80 (first hard disk)
MOV BX,0800 ; Set in combination with ES
INT 13 ; BIOS
JMP 10E ; Halt here
```

Fig. 5-2 Assembly program to read physical sector 0

Encrypted viruses present a slightly greater challenge to the researcher, as they have to be decrypted before being disassembled. This is sometimes quite tricky, since the virus writer may have used anti-DEBUG measures. Taking *Cascade* as an example, the decryption routine makes use of the Stack Pointer (SP). If the DEBUG breakpoint facility is used, the stack pointer must be valid and have at least 6 bytes available. Likewise, the target address will be modified by DEBUG to cause an INT 3H (one byte CC Hex instruction will be inserted there). *Cascade* uses SP, making it more difficult to use the breakpoint facility. Placing a breakpoint in the first encrypted instruction doesn't work, since the decryption routine in *Cascade* will decrypt the INT 3H instruction, producing a garbage byte. Analysing an encrypted virus is guaranteed to make one familiar with DEBUG.

Once the disassembled virus has been written out to a file (like VIR.ASM in the above example) the real fun begins. The analysis of the assembly code will reveal how the virus works, what it does and how it propagates. One should normally have available good PC documentation, which includes lists of interrupts (the *New Peter Norton Programmer's Guide to the IBM PC & PS/2* is suitable) and painstakingly work one's way through the disassembly, documenting instructions, interrupts and memory locations. The picture will soon start to emerge. The replicating part of the virus will be isolated as well as its payload. Any payload trigger conditions should be analysed very carefully, as these are easy to misinterpret (does it trigger on 12th or 13th day of the month ?).

Once the disassembly has been finished (or even before doing it) one can extract a hexadecimal pattern which can be used to search for the virus. 16 bytes are normally sufficient, provided that the pattern is chosen carefully so that it represents a fairly unique set of instructions, unlikely to be found in other executables.

Treat the disassembly as a confidential document and do not distribute it carelessly.

5.2.2 FORENSIC EVIDENCE

Every virus contains forensic evidence which could be used to trace its origin. Is it a derivative of another virus ? Does it contain any interesting messages ? Does it use a new replicating technique ? Which software tools were used to write it ?

5.2.2.1 Which Assembler ?

There are different ways of assembling 8086 family instructions, which produce identical results when executed. For example

```
XCHG BX,AX
```

could be assembled as 93 Hex, 87D8 Hex or 87C3 Hex. The result of the execution would be the same.

When the *Yale* virus was analysed, it was discovered that it had been assembled with the A86 assembler and not Microsoft's MASM.

5.2.2.2 Illegal Instructions

Some viruses contain instructions which are either not documented or not allowed by the target processor. Such instructions may execute correctly on the 8086 family processors, but will be trapped as illegal by the 80286 or 80386 processors.

There are several examples of this. The *Italian* virus uses the MOV CS,AX instruction (8EC8 Hex) which is executed properly by the 8086 processor, but trapped as an illegal instruction on 80286 and 80386 processors. Similarly, *Yale* uses the POP CS (0F Hex) instruction which executes correctly on an 8086, but is trapped as illegal on 80286 and 80386 processors.

5.2.2.3 Programming Style

Faced with the same programming task, ten programmers will program it in ten different ways. This is especially true in assembly language in which most PC viruses are written. PUSHing registers in a particular order onto the stack, using SHORT in JMP forward instructions, and other such constructs can all form a distinctive 'signature' of a programmer. Although this is difficult to quantify, looking at several programs written by the same person will give the researcher the feeling of *deja vu*.

Some time ago there was a debate on one of the bulletin boards as to whether the *dBASE* and *Typo* viruses were written by the same person. The programming style is certainly very similar; for example both viruses use an identical but unusual method to transfer control to the original program:

```
MOV AX,100H
JMP AX
```

There are also notable differences, such as the code used to modify interrupt 21H. The *dBASE* virus uses DOS INT 21H functions 35H and 25H, whereas *Typo* writes directly to memory.

Making judgements about programming style requires experience in the programming language concerned.

5.2.2.4 Language and Spelling

Viruses often have messages incorporated in the code and one can get strong clues to the country of origin of a virus by looking at the language (English, French, Icelandic), spelling (American-British), dates (Month-Day-Year or Day-Month-Year), ways of expressing oneself and so on.

For example, *Datacrime* virus contains the statement

```
RELEASED 1 MARCH 1989
```

This was almost certainly not written by an American and quite probably not by a Briton either (who would have written it as '1ST MARCH 1989'). An English-speaking European is a likely culprit. As another example, the *Fu Manchu* virus insults four politicians (Thatcher, Reagan, Botha and Waldheim). Calling someone 'a c***' is typically British and not used often in the USA. Another clue is offered by the positioning of the relevant strings within the virus. The Thatcher insult comes first, before Reagan, Botha or Waldheim. Would an American do that ? Probably not.

5.2.2.5 Place and Time of First Detection

Place and time of first detection of a virus can offer powerful clues as to its origins. This was how the *Italian* virus was tracked to the Polytechnic of Turin and *Jerusalem* to the Hebrew University in Jerusalem.

The speed of virus spread is much slower than most people expect. This means that the logging of occurrences is important, even with a significant margin of error in reporting the time of discovery. Place of discovery is more difficult to get wrong and can also be used in plotting the progress of the spread of a virus.

Electronic communications are making the plotting of the virus spread more difficult, since a user can contract a virus from a program downloaded from bulletin boards one mile away or 10,000 miles away equally easily.

5.2.2.6 Ancestors

Sometimes it is possible to determine the predecessors of a virus, since the authors have copied the majority of the code to produce a new virus (as was the case with *Fu Manchu*, which is a derivative of *Jerusalem*, or *Jerusalem* itself, which is a final version of a succession of viruses starting with *Suriv 1.01* and continuing with *Suriv 2.01* and *Suriv 3.00*). The author(s) of the series even preserved backwards compatibility, so that *Jerusalem* does not infect files already infected with *Suriv 1.01, Suriv 2.01* or *Suriv 3.00*. The author of *Fu Manchu* (almost certainly a different person) did not have to (or want to) support previous virus releases and this backward compatibility is absent from the *Fu Manchu*. This was pointed out by Joe Hirst in the August 1989 issue of the *Virus Bulletin*.

5.3 VIRUS MUTATIONS

Virus mutations occur when a captured virus is modified in some way. This is done by intentional assembly programming and is quite distinct from biological mutations, which occur accidentally.

5.3.1 CHANGING VIRUS SIDE-EFFECTS

A typical virus has some 500 to 1000 instructions, most of which form the self-replicating mechanism. Virus side-effects normally occupy only a small part of a virus, and are quite easy to change. It is feasible for a relatively inexperienced assembler programmer to modify an existing virus. Such a mutation could transform a comparatively harmless virus such as *Cascade*, into a destructive virus which erases the hard disk.

It is worth noting that **the complete destruction of data on the hard disk can be programmed in only 5 assembler instructions** and that modifying a known virus to do that could be done in a few minutes using DEBUG.

5.3.2 VIRUS 'IMPROVEMENTS'

There are several examples of improvements and corrections made to viruses. The *Cascade* virus in its original form has an infective length of 1701 bytes. It also exists in a version which has an infective length of 1704 bytes, which is a consequence of removing some superfluous branch instructions and introducing segment overrides. Whether that was done by the person who wrote the original isn't known. The *New Zealand* virus exists in two versions, where the second is a reorganised and tidied-up version of the first.

5.3.3 MUTATIONS TO FOOL PATTERN-CHECKING PROGRAMS

Pattern-checking programs rely on searching for a pattern known to exist within a virus. If a maliciously inclined person wanted to release a version of the virus which would not be recognised by the pattern checker, he could either change the order of instructions which are not dependent or implement the same effect using different instructions.

For example

```
MOV AX,7F00H
MOV BX,0
```

within a virus could be switched around to read

```
MOV BX,0
MOV AX,7F00H
```

Any pattern checker relying on the pattern produced by the first sequence of instructions (B800 7FBB 0000) would not recognise the mutated sequence (BB00 00B8 007F).

5.3.4 NEW VIRUSES

Sometimes the mutations of an existing virus will be so extensive that the virus will bear little resemblance to the original. Hex patterns extracted from the original are unlikely to be present in the new virus. *Fu Manchu* is, for example, such an extensive mutation of *Jerusalem*, that it is classed as a new virus.

5.4 VIRUS ATTACK STATISTICS

Virus attacks are rarely reported in the press, mainly because of the (legitimate) fear of bad publicity which an attack may bring to an organisation. The press have also a lot to answer for. The few organisations (in the UK) which **have** publicly admitted being victims have suffered from hounding and harassment from story-hungry journalists.

Organisations which have been affected by a virus usually prefer to lick their wounds alone and may consult an outside specialist after voluminous non-disclosure agreements have been signed.

As a result, it is impossible even to estimate how serious the virus problem is. The numbers of attacks are not reported anywhere, and various consultants who deal with virus attacks can only offer wild guesses as to the total extent of the problem.

The reporting of an infection is entirely up to the organisation in question, and as long as a stigma remains attached to infection, and infection in turn is related to poor security measures, nothing will change.

6

ANTI-VIRUS PROCEDURES - FIVE COUNTERMEASURES

With increasing well-being all people become aware,
sooner or later, that they have something to protect.

J. K. Galbraith, The Affluent Society

The fight against viruses involves the application of five countermeasures: **Preparation, Prevention, Detection, Containment** and **Recovery**.

6.1 PREPARATION

The following subsections outline what should be done **before** a virus attack occurs.

6.1.1 REGULAR AND SOUND BACKUPS

Backups are something which everybody should be doing in any case, but are especially important in case of an attack by a destructive virus. In case of data loss, the system can be restored as efficiently as possible. As part of the backup procedure, the master disks for all software (including the operating system) should be write-protected and stored in a safe place. This will enable a speedy restoration of any infected executables.

The backups should be **sound**, which means that there is little point in doing them **unless the data can actually be restored**. Backups should be tested frequently by performing complete restorations of the system.

6.1.2 WRITE-PROTECTED SYSTEM FLOPPY DISK

A write-protected system floppy disk should be prepared in advance and contain all system files plus AUTOEXEC.BAT, CONFIG.SYS and any other system files or device drivers such as ANSI.SYS. Note that CONFIG.SYS normally refers to other files which are loaded into memory before the system is started, using statements such as 'DEVICE=filename'. **All these files should be copied onto the floppy disk**, and CONFIG.SYS on the floppy should be modified, if necessary, to ensure that it refers to the files on the floppy disk, rather than the original copies on the hard disk.

If a computer becomes infected, this disk will be used to bootstrap the computer. This will ensure that various items on the computer can be examined through a 'clean' operating system, not giving the virus the chance to employ hiding techniques such as interrupt interception (see section 3.3: 'Virus Hiding Mechanisms').

This system disk **must be write-protected;** this is a hardware protection against the modification of any information on the disk. No virus, or for that matter, any software, can write to a write-protected floppy disk.

6.1.3 CONTINGENCY PLAN

This plan, which will be put into action in case of a virus attack, is usually part of the overall organisational security contingency plan and should include information on the following topics:

· The person within the organisation responsible for dealing with the attack and his deputy

· The consultant(s) outside the organisation who can (will) be called in to help with the attack

· Exact procedure for isolating infected disks and PCs

· Public Relations procedure to prevent unauthorised leaks about the attack spreading outside the organisation

6.2 PREVENTION

Preventing a virus from penetrating an organisation is equivalent to the military physically guarding their camps and states their frontiers. Medical parallels can also be drawn with only sterile surgical instruments allowed in an operating theatre.

The need to communicate introduces a potential virus entry path into any secure environment. Application software has to be purchased or updated, new operating systems installed, disks interchanged. The higher the volume of inbound traffic, the more opportunity a virus has of entering the environment.

The suppliers of executable code are potentially the most prolific places for distributing viruses. Most users assume that the code received from reputable companies is virus-free and any anti-virus barriers will be promptly raised when such an executable arrives on the doorstep. Most software companies do realise their potential as sources of virus infection and take appropriate countermeasures.

Three practical techniques exist to strengthen the fence: **creating user awareness**, implementing **hygiene rules** and providing a **'dirty' PC**.

6.2.1 CREATING USER AWARENESS

Creating user awareness is a very important factor in establishing an effective virus prevention policy. Users must be made aware that execution of unauthorised software (such as demonstration disks and games) can lead to virus penetration of the best guarded environment and consequent losses to the organisation.

The problems are similar to the ones faced by the Government in persuading drug addicts not to share needles. While most computer users **do** behave sensibly and obey the rules, there will always be some who go on playing illegally copied games and other software on company computers and exposing the whole organisation to risk. As the AIDS disk scare showed, a number of people are happy to install **anything** on their PC, showing a blind trust in the creators of any software.

Strengthening awareness is a matter of commonsense and measures include the use of leaflets, posters, virus demonstrations, presentations and so on.

6.2.2 HYGIENE RULES

The observance of **hygiene** is by far the most effective way of preventing a virus attack. A virus program has little chance of reaching a computer if that computer is not networked, has a limited number of users (preferably only one), and is never used with disks from other sources. If one can possibly avoid it, one should not use programs taken from bulletin boards, pirated, or borrowed from a friend of a friend.

The list of rules is straightforward and it essentially boils down to the fact that every executable item which is to run on a computer should be treated with suspicion. This includes **free demonstration disks**, **shareware**, **public domain** and **bulletin board software**. A simple example set of rules is:

· Do not use software 'pulled down' from bulletin boards. A number of bulletin boards in the UK and the USA offer free software which can be downloaded by modem. With a few noteworthy exceptions, little control and checking is done on these programs and their potential for carrying a virus is high.

· Do not use shareware. Similar reasoning to the bulletin board software applies. A copy of the shareware program you get is the 10th or the 50th copy and the probability and risk of the program picking up a virus before it has reached you is high. There are a few shareware companies which claim to distribute 'original' packages, straight from the author. The likelihood of a virus infection is lower, although one would have to examine each individual author's anti-virus precautions in order to be absolutely certain.

· Use only programs from reputable manufacturers. A reputable manufacturer will implement anti-virus security procedures on its development computers to ensure that no virus is embedded in a program at that stage. There **has** been a case where a manufacturer distributed infected copies of the software, but that was an isolated incident which opened up peoples' eyes and highlighted the need for strict QA (Quality Assurance) procedures. Manufacturers will normally supply software on write-protected disks, which greatly decreases the chances of a virus infection after the disk has left the manufacturer's premises. Shrink-wrapping the software or placing the software in a sealed-envelope ensures that you are the first person to use that copy of the original disk.

6.2.3 DIRTY PC

A dirty PC is a physically isolated machine, not connected to networks, which can be used for trying out new software, playing games and essentially doing anything which would be dangerous to do on a machine used for day-to-day work. If the dirty PC does not already exist in the organisation, it should be provided.

Employees should be encouraged to use it to try out any unauthorised software coming from outside, including demo disks and games. No company work should ever be done on that machine, and any disks used on the dirty PC should not be used in any other computer. Anti-virus software should be run as often as possible to check this machine for virus presence.

This concept is a very powerful tool against viruses, although it can be difficult to 'sell' to management if budgets and resources are strained. As PC prices are constantly going down, the low cost of a dirty PC (which need not be the latest model and can be second-hand) should be treated as part of an insurance policy against virus attack.

6.3 DETECTION

Should a virus penetrate the initial obstacles placed in its way, there should exist a reliable way of detecting its presence before its side-effects are triggered.

The detection should not rely on the user's observation; for example noticing that the file size has changed (Fig. 3-4) or that the amount of available memory has decreased (Fig. 6-1). Detection is best done by one of the anti-virus software packages (see chapter 7: 'Anti-Virus Software'). As with any other security requirements, the effectivenes of any such measure is of paramount importance and must take precedence over user convenience. However, user convenience must not be neglected,

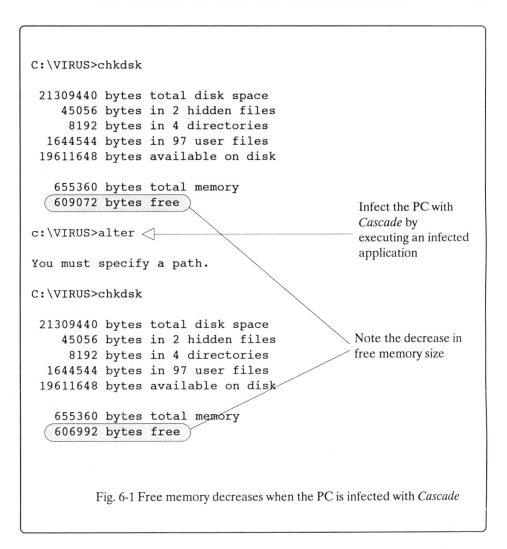

```
C:\VIRUS>chkdsk

 21309440 bytes total disk space
    45056 bytes in 2 hidden files
     8192 bytes in 4 directories
  1644544 bytes in 97 user files
 19611648 bytes available on disk

   655360 bytes total memory
   609072 bytes free

c:\VIRUS>alter

You must specify a path.

C:\VIRUS>chkdsk

 21309440 bytes total disk space
    45056 bytes in 2 hidden files
     8192 bytes in 4 directories
  1644544 bytes in 97 user files
 19611648 bytes available on disk

   655360 bytes total memory
   606992 bytes free
```

Infect the PC with *Cascade* by executing an infected application

Note the decrease in free memory size

Fig. 6-1 Free memory decreases when the PC is infected with *Cascade*

as any security measure which makes life difficult for the user is likely at some stage to be circumvented.

6.3.1 'STRANGE' OCCURRENCES

Sometimes users will notice 'strange' things happening, such as programs taking longer to load than usual, a disk light flashing when it should not be, program size varying or free memory size decreasing. All these occurrences could point to a virus attack, but they should not be relied upon for detecting virus presence. They rely too much on the subjective powers of observation of an individual to be usable in a reliable way.

6.3.2 RECOGNITION OF A CAPTURED VIRUS

Once a virus has been detected, one needs a reliable and quick way of recognising it. A pattern check will verify only one part of the virus, while one could be dealing with a mutation containing a pattern belonging to the original virus. The side-effects of a mutated virus can be completely different to the ones in the original.

6.3.2.1 Parasitic Viruses

In order to establish a positive identification of a parasitic virus, set up a dirty PC and make two copies of the same 'sacrificial goat' executable. Infect one executable using the newly discovered virus and the other using the original virus. Run the DOS COMP command. If there are no differences, the virus is the same as the one already in captivity. If the differences are discovered, the virus could still be the same, but it could be encrypted or self-modifying. This will have to be analysed more closely using DEBUG and the disassembly techniques outlined in the section 5.2: 'Dissection of a Captured Virus'.

6.3.2.2 Boot Sector Viruses

To identify a boot sector virus positively, do a similar experiment as with a parasitic virus. Format two identical floppy disks, and on a dirty PC infect one with the new virus and the other one with the original virus. Run DOS DISKCOMP (this can be done even on a single drive machine) to compare the contents of the two disks. If there are no differences, the virus is the same as the original. If there are differences, the virus could still be the same, but it could either be encrypted, self-modifying or use randomly selected sectors for storing the bulk of its code. This will warrant further analysis.

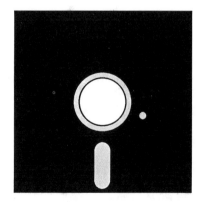

Fig. 6-2a Write-unprotected 5 1/4" disk   Fig. 6-2b Write-protected 5 1/4" disk

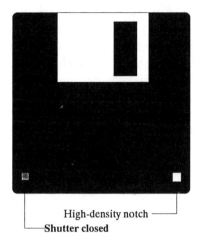

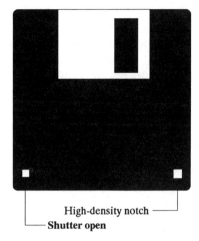

High-density notch ——————   High-density notch ——————
——Shutter closed   └— Shutter open

Fig. 6-3a Write-**un**protected 3 1/2" disk   Fig. 6-3b Write-protected 3 1/2" disk

6.4 CONTAINMENT

Once a virus is detected, infected PCs and disks have to be identified and isolated.

A contingency plan prepared in advance will be extremely valuable at the moment of virus discovery. Panic invariably results and a point-by-point checklist makes it more difficult to skip an important item.

6.4.1 NETWORK ACCESS

Depending on where on the network the virus has been discovered, the type of the network and the type of the virus, one may take the decision to disconnect the PCs physically from the network. This, however, is not usually necessary.

6.4.2 DISK INTERCHANGE

Any unauthorised disk interchange between PCs should be temporarily suspended. **Masking tape placed over disk drives is a good physical indicator that disk drives should not be used.**

6.4.3 WRITE-PROTECT TABS

All floppy disks which are not purposefully intended to be infected, should be protected with write-protect tabs. On 5 1/4" disks (Fig. 6-2) the application of the write-protect tab means that nothing can be written to that disk. On 3 1/2" disks (Fig. 6-3) the appearance of a window on the sliding shutter signifies that the disk is write-protected.

Write-protection on disks is a hardware function and no amount of software manipulation can persuade the hardware to change its mind and write to the disk.

A word of caution: A number of (conflicting) reports have been published regarding the (in)effectiveness of silver (or black) write-protect tabs on 5 1/4" disks. This is true on some older drives which used a mirror under the floppy disk notch to reflect the light back to the photo-sensitive element next to the light source (Fig. 6-4). Placing a silver (or a shiny black) write-protect tab is the same as bringing the mirror closer to the light source, which makes the drive believe that the disk is not write-protected. Unfortunately, some reports have wrongly indicated that the **matt** tabs are the culprits, which resulted in a spectacular confusion at various sites.

The best rule is that, if in doubt, try copying a file onto a disk write-protected using a tab of your favourite colour. I use **matt black tabs**, which have never caused any problems.

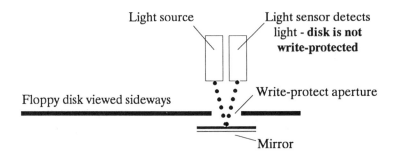

Fig. 6-4a Floppy disk is not write-protected

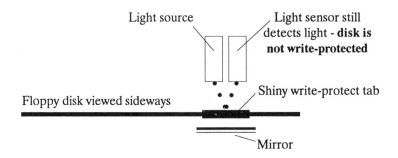

Fig. 6-4b Floppy disk **not** 'write-protected' with a silver tab

6.5 RECOVERY

Recovery from a virus attack involves **two main stages**:

(1) Elimination of the virus from the infected PC hard disks and floppy disks, and

(2) Recovery from the effect of any virus side-effects

6.5.1 ELIMINATION OF THE VIRUS FROM INFECTED PCS

To eliminate the virus from the infected hard disk, each PC should be bootstrapped from a **write-protected system floppy disk** (see section 6.1: 'Preparation') and any infected objects (bootstrap sectors, executables) on the hard disk replaced with clean copies. This can be done by the 'brute force' method of reformatting the disk and reloading the clean copies of all executables, or, alternatively, selectively replacing infected objects. The former method will lose all data files on disk, while the latter is more prone to errors and subsequent reinfections. Data (but not the executables) can usually be backed up safely from the disk for subsequent use, but the backing program must be run from an uninfected disk and must not be infected itself.

A copy of *Norton Utilities* or *PC Tools* can be of great help at this stage.

Software specifically designed to 'remove' a virus from executable images should not be used (see 'Virus Removal and Innoculation Software'). This is a risky procedure akin to trying to use tweezers to remove bacteria from an egg infected with salmonella, so that the egg can be eaten. It is much better to discard the egg completely and not try the risky approach of bacteria removal.

To clear infected floppy disks, a pattern-matching program should be run on each floppy, in order to discover whether it contains any virus code. After any valuable data has been backed up in a way similar to that outlined for hard disks, infected floppies should be discarded (reformatted - FORMAT A:).

Reinfection often occurs after the 'cleanup' has been completed, sometimes minutes after completion. Although thoroughness will reduce the likelihood of reinfection, one should be prepared for the eventuality.

In the process of eliminating the virus, do not forget to preserve a copy in a safe place, on a clearly marked disk, for detailed analysis.

6.5.2 RECOVERY FROM VIRUS SIDE-EFFECTS

Recovery from virus side-effects depends on the virus. In the case of innocuous viruses such as *Cascade,* recovery from side-effects is obviously not necessary, while in the case of a virus like *Datacrime*, recovery will involve the restoration of a complete hard disk.

6.5.3 OTHER POINTS

There are a few other points to consider when performing the recovery from a virus attack.

· Discover and close loopholes which caused the virus to enter the organisation.

· Inform any possible recipients of the infected disks outside the organisation that they may be affected by the virus.

· Consider the implications to the organisation of the bad publicity.

7

ANTI-VIRUS SOFTWARE

You know my method. It is founded upon the observance of trifles.

Lady Cardine Douglas-Home, The Boscombe Valley Mystery

The emergence of a virus threat has been closely followed by the mushrooming of various software packages designed to combat viruses. The users are faced with a bewildering choice in trying to pick the best package which will be effective against something they have never seen, and do not particularly wish to see. How do they test it ? What should they use and why ?

7.1 ANTI-VIRUS SOFTWARE TYPES

The many anti-virus software packages on the market can be divided into two categories: **Virus non-specific** and **Virus specific.** Each category can, in turn, be divided into two sub-categories, as shown in Fig. 7-1.

Virus non-specific	Virus specific
Checksumming software	Scanning software
Monitoring software	Monitoring software

Fig. 7-1 Anti-virus software types

7.1.1 CHECKSUMMING SOFTWARE

Checksumming software relies on the calculation of a checksum of any executable on the system followed by periodic recalculations in order to verify that the checksum has not changed. If a virus attacks an executable, it will have to change at least one bit inside the executable, which will result in a completely different checksum.

This type of software is reactive rather than proactive, in that a virus attack will be detected **after** it happens. The program FINGER listed in appendix C is an example of virus non-specific checksumming software.

Checksumming software also relies on the fact that the executables are 'clean' (i.e. virus-free) before the initial checksumming is applied. This can be ensured by doing one of the following:

1. Initialising the PC by performing a low-level format of the hard disk and downloading all software from manufacturers' original disks.

and/or

2. Using virus-specific scanning software to check the system for the presence of any known viruses.

The checksumming approach is the only known method which will detect all viruses, present and future, with absolute certainty. This makes it inherently desirable as a **long-term anti-virus strategy** in any organisation.

The method of performing the checksumming process (the checksumming algorithm) is very important. Three general approaches are possible:

1. Simple checksums

2. Cyclic Redundancy Checks (CRCs)

3. Cryptographically strong checksums

The results of the checksumming algorithm must not be easily reproducible (lest a virus should do this on infection, preventing its detection), which eliminates the first two. **Cryptographically strong checksums are the only approach which should be used.**

7.1.2 SCANNING SOFTWARE

A virus-scanning program relies on the knowledge of known virus 'patterns'. When a new virus appears in the wild, it is analysed, and a characteristic pattern of some 10 to 16 bytes recorded. The virus-scanning program will scan all executables on a disk, including the operating system and the bootstrap sector(s), and compare their contents with the known virus patterns.

The program SEARCH listed in appendix B is an example of a virus-specific scanning software.

Of course, this type of software can only discover viruses that it 'knows' about and as such has to be continually updated with new patterns, as new viruses appear. This is the main problem with this type of software. At the moment there is no national or international databank of virus patterns, but the creation of such an institution may be beneficial for the future. A full list of viruses and their hexadecimal patterns is published monthly by the *Virus Bulletin*.

The length of the virus pattern is also of crucial importance. If a short pattern is used, the chances are that the scanning software will produce a number of false positives, finding the pattern in completely innocent software. If a long pattern is used, false positives will be reduced, but on the other hand the incidence of false negatives will be increased since any virus mutation will have a better chance of not matching the pattern, and, hence, slipping through the net. This is especially true with encrypting viruses.

Most scanning software is slow, although it is possible to speed the search for viruses by not looking at **all** locations, but only at the locations known to be infected by a specific virus. Unfortunately, this complicates both the scanning software and the list of viruses, which becomes more difficult to keep up to date **and absolutely correct**, thus increasing the risk of false negatives. It is because of this that this approach is appropriate and practical only in special circumstances.

Scanning software is especially useful for checking incoming floppy disks for the presence of known viruses.

7.1.3 MONITORING SOFTWARE

Monitoring software packages (also called on-line packages) install themselves as memory-resident *TSR* (terminate-stay-resident) programs in a manner similar to some PC utilities like Borland's *Sidekick*. They intercept and monitor disk I/O, trying either to monitor system integrity or to detect 'virus activity'.

While this approach is attractive in theory, there is unfortunately no fixed 'set of rules' regarding what a virus should or should not do. As a result, false alarms can result from legitimate program activity which is misinterpreted by the anti-virus software (this in turn usually leads to users ignoring all warnings!). Conversely, any virus which does not comply with the monitoring program's concept of virus activity will be ignored. The monitoring activity also degrades system performance and can be incompatible with network software, certain application programs and so on.

The greatest drawback of memory-resident products, however, is that **any intelligent virus program can easily bypass or disable them**. The mechanism used by anti-virus software for intercepting disk reads and writes, i.e. to change the vectors in the DOS interrupt table, is exactly that used by most virus programs.

On computer architectures with mechanisms such as memory ownership, hardware memory protection and privileged instruction sets, memory-resident products can theoretically be implemented in a secure manner. Since these features are not available on Intel 8086/88 processors or the MS-DOS operating system, memory-resident products are not suitable for any serious use on PCs.

7.1.4 OTHER ANTI-VIRUS SOFTWARE

7.1.4.1 Integrity Shells

Integrity shells deserve a special mention, since they are a comparatively new development in anti-virus software. The idea behind them is that a layer is added above the DOS command level, so that the shell 'filters-through' any request to execute a program. Before executing the program, the anti-virus part of the shell will perform an on-line checksumming of the executable and compare it with the precomputed value. If the values do not agree, the execution of the program will not be commenced.

Although the integrity shell concept is very appealing, it is not possible to implement it in a secure way under the MS-DOS operating system. MS-DOS recognises only one type of machine instructions and any program can do anything, including bypassing the shell and rendering its protection useless. Integrity shells are more secure under operating systems like Unix, VMS or OS/2, where inter-process separation is well defined and where the execution of a 'dangerous' instruction (in operating system terms), will cause the offending process to be suspended.

Some integrity shells combine the integrity checking function with virus-monitoring software, so that any suspicious activity is reported. Numerous false alarms invariably result and tend to be ignored after some time. The user is unfortunately left with a false sense of security, which is probably the worst result of using such products.

Integrity shells have a great potential under OS/2 or Xenix operating systems, while their use under MS-DOS is not recommended.

7.1.4.2 Access-control Products

Some access-control products are marketed as 'virus protection' devices. One computer manufacturer even markets their personal computers as 'virus-proof', using the argument that no unauthorised software can be installed on the PC due to the built-in access control package.

The truth is that the virus protection offered by access control products is often very limited. Just like monitoring software which intercepts certain interrupts, access control products will try to block writing to executables, writing to disk sectors and other similar actions, **but will only achieve this if the writing is attempted via DOS or BIOS calls**. Any access which is done 'hands-on' will not be detected and cannot be intercepted.

Encryption, used in some access control products, can go some way towards preventing direct hardware read access; a virus will not be able to read or write in a DOS-legal fashion directly to and from a disk which has been encrypted using a custom key. However, it is feasible to design a virus which will bypass most, if not all access control products which use interrupt interception as the means of controlling disk operations.

One benefit of using access control products is that they prevent the installation of unauthorised executables onto the system or their execution from the floppy disk drive. This means that a normal user cannot run a potentially infectious application, but no such protection extends to a user with supervisor privileges.

7.1.5 VIRUS-REMOVAL AND 'INOCULATION' SOFTWARE

There exists software on the market which attempts to remove viruses from infected disks and infected programs. This is not something to be recommended, as it is not an easy operation in the majority of cases. Mistakes are possible, if not probable. It is much more straight forward to replace the infected programs with manufacturers' originals.

Likewise, 'inoculation' software which labels disks or executables in such a way that a particular virus will not infect them is **not to be used**. This software introduces a virus signature into objects it wants to protect, leading the virus to believe that the object is already infected. Apart from the fact that such 'protection' can only be done against one, or at most a few viruses, it is not a long term solution and can introduce a false sense of security.

One widely recommended "inoculation" technique against the *Italian* virus, actually involved the corruption of the operating system tables.

7.2 TESTING ANTI-VIRUS PRODUCTS

It is strongly recommended that only tested anti-virus products are used. The testing should be done for **usability** as well as **security**.

The security aspect of testing is a rather specialist task which cannot be done by the average user. Most users have never encountered, nor have any desire to encounter highly infectious and harmful viruses on their system. They do not wish to risk their valuable data just in order to ascertain the effectiveness of anti-virus software. The testing of anti-virus software should be done in a controlled environment, by experts. Testing against a large selection of viruses is not necessarily the main requirement, since testing against **a well chosen sample of viruses** can reveal a lot.

The testing for usability should be done by the purchaser on his own typical hardware and software configuration.

7.3 SUMMARY OF ANTI-VIRUS SOFTWARE

In summary, the recommended long-term approach is to use **virus non-specific checksumming software, based on cryptographic checksums**. This will allow convenient everyday checking of system integrity, secure against any present or future viruses.

In addition, there are situations in which **virus-specific scanning software can be useful**, provided its limitations are clearly understood.

Monitoring software should not be used as it cannot be made effective against all viruses and can lull the user into a false sense of security. **The same applies to virus-removal** and **'inoculation' software** for similar reasons.

The advantages of the non-memory-resident approach over memory-resident products are considerable. Above all, the operation can be made fully secure through both bootstrapping the computer and running the anti-virus software from a write-protected floppy disk. Furthermore there is no performance degradation or incompatibility with other software in normal operation, and anti-virus checks can be scheduled or integrated into other procedures as required.

A

BIBLIOGRAPHY AND OTHER SOURCES OF INFORMATION

There are three golden rules for writing a good book.
Unfortunately no-one knows what they are.

W. Somerset Maugham

A.1 BOOKS ON VIRUSES AND RELATED ISSUES

80386 Programmer's Reference Manual, *Intel Corporation*

Computer Viruses, Peers, E., Ennis, C., *Deloitte Haskins & Sells*

Computer Viruses, A High Tech Disease, Burger, R., *Abacus*

Computer Viruses, What They Are, How They Work, and How to Avoid Them, Windcrest J. L., *Mayo*

Data & Computer Security, Dictionary of Standards Concepts and Terms, Longley, D., Shain, M., *Macmillan*

Data Security Reference Guide, *Sophos Ltd.*

Datapro Reports on Microcomputer Security, *McGraw-Hill*

iAPX 86,88 User's Manual, *Intel Corporation*

Microsoft Macro Assembler 5.1, *Microsoft*

Peter Norton Programmer's Guide to IBM PC & PS/2, Norton, P. and Wilton, R., *Micosoft Press*

The Complete Computer Virus Handbook, Frost, D., Beale, I., Frost, C., *Price Waterhouse and Pitman*

The Computer Virus Crisis, Fites, P., Johnston, P., Kratz, M., *Van Nostrand Reinhold*

The Computer Virus Handbook, Highland, H. J., *Elsevier Advanced Technology*

Technical Reference for IBM Personal Computer AT, *IBM*, No. 6280070

Technical Reference for IBM Personal Computer XT, *IBM*, No. 6280089

A.2 PERIODICALS ON VIRUSES AND DATA SECURITY

Computer Fraud and Security Bulletin, *Elsevier Advanced Technology*, 256 Banbury Road, Oxford, OX2 7DH, England, Tel. (0865) 512242

Computer Law and Practice, *Frank Cass & Co. Ltd.*, Gainsborough House, 11 Gainsborough Road, London E11 1RS, England, Tel. (01) 530 4226

The Computer Law and Security Report, Law Department, *Southampton University*, Southampton, SO9 5NH, England, Tel. (0703) 559122

Computers & Security, *Elsevier Advanced Technology*, 256 Banbury Road, Oxford, OX2 7DH, England, Tel. (0865) 512242

Datenschutz Berater, POB 2157, 5024 Pulheim, West Germany, Tel. +49 22 348 2227

Enigma Variations, *Osprey Media*, 67 Linden Lea, Garston, Watford, WD2 7DW, England, Tel. (0923) 675052

Information Security Monitor, *IBC Technical Services*, Bath House, 56 Holborn Viaduct, London EC1A 2EX, England, Tel. (01) 236 4080

Virus Bulletin, *Virus Bulletin Ltd*, Haddenham, Aylesbury, Buckinghamshire, HP17 8JD, England, Tel. (0844) 290396

A.3 ELECTRONIC BULLETIN BOARDS CARRYING VIRUS-RELATED DISCUSSIONS

BIX is a bulletin board run by the Byte magazine in the US. On-line subscription is possible on 617-861-9767 (full duplex, 8 bits, no parity, 1 stop bit or 7 bits, even parity, 1 stop bit). Hit the Return key, on *login* prompt enter *bix* and on *Name?* prompt enter *bix.flatfee*. Credit cards are accepted. Packet Switch Network (PSS) address is 310690157800. A number of virus-related conferences are going on; try *law/virus* and *security/critters*.

CIX is a London-based bulletin board which carries regular discussions on a number of security-related topics, including viruses. To register, telephone 01 399 5252 (any modem speed). Payment by credit card accepted.

The author can be contacted via CIX (username *husky*).

B

'SEARCH' VIRUS-SPECIFIC DETECTION PROGRAM

My father believed in smiting sin wherever he found it;
what I complained of was that he always seemed to find it in the same place.

Saki (H. H. Munro) and Charles Maude, The Watched Pot

This appendix contains the source code for a virus-specific detection program called SEARCH which scans the currently logged-in drive for the hexadecimal virus patterns read in from the file SEARCH.PAT.

Virus patterns have to be updated frequently with the latest virus patterns. Section 4.2 contains the list of virus patterns known by January 1990, which can and should be constantly updated. One of the sources of virus patterns is the monthly *Virus Bulletin*, listed in appendix A.

The program is not particularly robust in error-handling, which had to be sacrificed for brevity. It is also not particularly fast; enhancing both shortcomings should prove a useful exercise for a competent C programmer.

B.1 DESCRIPTION OF SEARCH

The SEARCH program is a virus-specific detection program which scans **the currently logged-in drive** for the presence of known viruses. The virus patterns are read-in from the file SEARCH.PAT which has to reside on the disk in the current drive.

By default, SEARCH will scan COM, EXE, SYS and OVL files recursively (i.e. from the root directory downward, visiting every subdirectory in turn). In addition to that, it will also scan the partition bootstrap sector 0, as well as the disk bootstrap sector on the first hard disk (logical drive 80H). The user can specify file(s) to be scanned in the command line. For example, if you want to scan all BIN files instead of the default files, enter

```
SEARCH *.BIN
```

You can enter more than one file descriptor in the command line. For example

```
SEARCH SUSPECT.BIN ONEMORE.BIN
```

would search the files SUSPECT.BIN and ONEMORE.BIN for the presence of viruses.

Virus patterns are read in from the file SEARCH.PAT. Any text between a semicolon ';' and the end of the line is ignored. Every pattern has a pattern name of up to 16 characters, followed by up to 16 bytes in hexadecimal. Spaces and TAB characters can be used for clarity. For example

```
Virus_1 3E 6B 78 78 00 90 ; This is a comment
; The above is the pattern for Virus 1
Virus_2 ab39 9823 278f fffe 890f
```

defines two virus patterns: Virus_1 and Virus_2, the first one consisting of 6 bytes and the second one of 10 bytes.

Remember that SEARCH can only detect viruses about which it knows. You should make sure that SEARCH.PAT is kept up to date with the patterns of new and mutated viruses.

B.2 COMPILING SEARCH

The majority of SEARCH code is written in 'C', but some routines call BIOS and DOS and are written in assembly language. The 'C' code can be compiled by most compilers, but it has been tested only using Aztec C by Manx Software Systems Inc. The assembly language routines assume that they will be called from Aztec C and if you are using a different compiler, make sure that you use the correct calling procedure and preserve the right registers.

Aztec C assumes that AX, BX, CX, and DX registers will not be preserved, while BP, SP, SI and DI will. Microsoft C, for example, assumes that SI, DI, BP, SS and DS will be saved.

Some compiler libraries contain the BIOS and DOS calling routines directly from C and so the whole SEARCH software can be written in C.

Note that SEARCH code in assembly language is also used by the FINGER program presented in appendix C.

Some compilers (like Aztec) provide the make facility similar to Unix make. This simplifies the preparation of any software. The makefile for SEARCH modules is listed below:

```
searchas.o: searchas.asm
search.o: search.c
SEARCH=search.o searchas.o
search: search.exe
@echo search made
search.exe: $(SEARCH)
ln $(SEARCH) -lc
```

To compile SEARCH, type

```
make search
```

and the computer will do the rest.

B.3 SEARCH CODE IN 'C'

The C code for SEARCH should be entered into one file called SEARCH.C. The FINGER program in appendix C can be used to verify the correctness of the code. The fingerprint for SEARCH.C is AB1E3AD5 (remember to run FINGER with the -N option):

```
FINGER -N SEARCH.C
```

File SEARCH.C:

```
/*
   This utility will search a system for known viruses
*/

#include "libc.h"
#include "fcntl.h"

#define EOF (-1)

#define FALSE (0)
#define TRUE (!FALSE)

#define NORMAL_EXIT 0
#define ERROR_EXIT (-1)

#define NO_ERROR 0
#define ERROR (-2)

#define BUFSIZE 2048*2     /* of buff[] */
#define MAX_BUFF 1024    /* used when fingerprinting absolute sectors */

#define MAX_LINE 128
#define MAXRECURSIVE 128

#define SEARCH_PAT "SEARCH.PAT"
```

```c
#define MAX_PATTERNS 256
#define MAX_NAME 16
#define MAX_PATTERN_LENGTH 16
struct patt{
   char name[MAX_NAME]; /* name of the virus */
   int bytes_in_pattern; /* how many bytes are in pattern */
   unsigned char pattern[MAX_PATTERN_LENGTH];
} patterns[MAX_PATTERNS];
static int max_patterns=0;
static int pattern_line=0;

struct ms_dos_buff{
   char reserved[21]; /* for MS-DOS use on subsequent find_nexts */
   unsigned char attr; /* attribute found */
   unsigned int time;
   unsigned int date;
   unsigned int size_l; /* low size */
   unsigned int size_h; /* high size */
   char pname[13]; /* packed name */
};

struct{
   int drive;
   unsigned available_clusters;
   unsigned clusters_per_drive;
   unsigned bytes_per_sector;
   unsigned sectors_per_cluster;
} disk_space;

struct dir_list {
   char *dir_path_and_name;
   struct dir_list *next;
} root;

#define OVERLAP (MAX_PATTERN_LENGTH-1)
static unsigned char buff[BUFSIZE+OVERLAP];

static int patterns_discovered=0;
static int err=0;
static long int total_bytes_searched=0l;

void nonrecursive_search_files();
void recursive_search_files();
void invert_pattern();

void do_path();
void complete_search_buff();
void complete_search_file();
void add_dir_to_list();

void search_partition_boot_sector();
void search_boot_sector();

unsigned int getdosversion();
unsigned int absread();
unsigned int lowdiskread();

void stradd();

char *malloc();

main(argc,argv)
int argc;
char *argv[];
```

```
{
   register int i;

   if(read_patterns()==ERROR) exit(ERROR_EXIT);
   if(max_patterns) printf("Searching for %d patterns.\n",max_patterns);
   else{
      printf("You must specify patterns in SEARCH.PAT file\n");
      exit(ERROR_EXIT);
   }

   if(argc>1) for(i=1;i<argc;i++){
      if(*argv[i]=='-') switch(*(argv[i]+1)){
      default:
         printf("SEARCH will search the current drive for known viruses.\n");
         printf("Virus patterns have to be specified in SEARCH.PAT.\n\n");
         printf("You can name specific groups of files to be searched in the command
line,\nfor example:\n\n");
         printf("\tSEARCH *.EXE\n");
         exit(ERROR_EXIT);
      } else{
         nonrecursive_search_files(argv[i]);
         continue;
      }
   } else{
      recursive_search_files("\\*.COM");
      recursive_search_files("\\*.EXE");
      recursive_search_files("\\*.SYS");
      recursive_search_files("\\*.OVL");
      search_partition_boot_sector();
      search_boot_sector();
   }

   if(err) printf("%d error(s) encountered during searching.\n",err);

   printf("%ld bytes searched.\n",total_bytes_searched);

   if(patterns_discovered) printf("%d virus pattern(s)
discovered.\n",patterns_discovered);
   else printf("No virus patterns discovered.\n");

   exit(NORMAL_EXIT);
}


void nonrecursive_search_files(pattern)
char pattern[];
{
   register int i,j;
   struct ms_dos_buff buf;
   char s[MAXRECURSIVE];

   strcpy(s,pattern);

   for(j=strlen(s)-1;j>=0;j--)
      if(s[j]=='\\') break;

   i=getfirst(pattern,0xffe7,&buf); /* no Dir / Vol */

   for(;i==0;i=getnext()){
      strcpy(s+j+1,buf.pname);
      complete_search_file(s);
   }
}
```

```
void recursive_search_files(pattern)
char pattern[];
{
   char init_path[MAXRECURSIVE],descriptor[MAXRECURSIVE];
   char local_path[MAXRECURSIVE];

   strcpy(init_path,"\\");
   strcpy(descriptor,pattern);
   root.next=NULL;

   do_path(init_path,descriptor);
   while(find_dir(local_path)) do_path(local_path,descriptor);
}


void do_path(path,descriptor)
char path[],descriptor[];
{
   register int i;
   char drive_and_path[MAXRECURSIVE],local_path[MAXRECURSIVE];
   struct ms_dos_buff buf;

   strcpy(drive_and_path,path);
   if(drive_and_path[strlen(drive_and_path)-1]=='\\') stradd(drive_and_path,"*.*");
   else stradd(drive_and_path,"\\*.*");

   i=getfirst(drive_and_path,0xffff,&buf);

   for(;i==0;i=getnext()){ /* collect directories */
      if(buf.attr&0x10){ /* Dir */
         if(!strcmp(buf.pname,".") || !strcmp(buf.pname,"..")) continue;
         strcpy(local_path,path);
         if(local_path[strlen(local_path)-1]!='\\') stradd(local_path,"\\");
         stradd(local_path,buf.pname);
         add_dir_to_list(local_path);
      } /* ignore anything which is not a dir */
   }

   drive_and_path[strlen(drive_and_path)-3]='\0'; /* get rid of *.* */
   if(descriptor[0]=='\\') stradd(drive_and_path,descriptor+1);
   else stradd(drive_and_path,descriptor);

   i=getfirst(drive_and_path,0xffe7,&buf); /* ignore Dir/Vol */

   for(;i==0;i=getnext()){
      strcpy(local_path,path);
      if(local_path[strlen(local_path)-1]!='\\') stradd(local_path,"\\");
      stradd(local_path,buf.pname);
      complete_search_file(local_path);
   }
}


void add_dir_to_list(s)
char s[];
{
   struct dir_list *nextp;

   for(nextp = &root;nextp->next;nextp=nextp->next);
   if(nextp->next=(struct dir_list *) malloc(sizeof(root))){
      nextp=nextp->next;
```

```
        if(nextp->dir_path_and_name=malloc((unsigned)(strlen(s)+1))){
          strcpy(nextp->dir_path_and_name,s);
          nextp->next=NULL;
          return;
        } else{
          printf("Too many directories to store in memory\n");
          exit(ERROR_EXIT);
        }
    } else{
      printf("Too many directories\n");
      exit(ERROR_EXIT);
    }
}


void search_partition_boot_sector()
{
    disk_space.drive=currentdisk()+1; /* get current disk drive */
    bytesfree(&disk_space); /* will get drive parameters */

    printf("Checking partition boot sector of drive %c:\n",disk_space.drive+'A'-1);

    if(absread(disk_space.drive-1,buff,1,0)){
      printf("Could not read partition boot sector\n");
      err++;
      return;
    }
    complete_search_buff(0,buff,0,disk_space.bytes_per_sector-1);
}


void search_boot_sector()
{
    register int i;
    unsigned int drive,head,cylinder,sector;

    drive=0x80; /* first hard disk */
    head=0;
    cylinder=0;
    sector=1; /* location of the boot sector */

    printf("Checking disk boot sector of disk drive number %02x\n",drive);

    for(i=0;i<MAX_BUFF;i++) buff[i]=0x00;


if(lowdiskread((head<<8)|(drive&0xff),buff,(cylinder<<8)|((cylinder>>2)&0xc0)|(sector&0x3f))){
      printf("Could not read boot sector\n");
      err++;
      return;
    }

    complete_search_buff(1,buff,0,MAX_BUFF-1);
}


void complete_search_buff(what,buff,from_byte,to_byte)
int what;
unsigned char buff[];
int from_byte,to_byte;
{
    register unsigned int j;
    register int i,k;
```

```
      total_bytes_searched+=to_byte-from_byte;

   for(j=from_byte;j<=to_byte;j++){
      for(i=0;i<max_patterns;i++){
         if((patterns[i].pattern)[0]!=buff[j]) continue; /* not in */
         if(patterns[i].bytes_in_pattern>j-from_byte+1) continue; /* out of boundary
*/

         for(k=1;k<patterns[i].bytes_in_pattern;k++)
            if((patterns[i].pattern)[k]!=buff[j-k]) break;
         if(k<patterns[i].bytes_in_pattern) continue; /* not in */

         switch(what){
         case 0:
            printf("Virus '%s' found in partition boot sector starting at the address
%04x\n",patterns[i].name,j-k+1);
            break;
         case 1:
            printf("Virus '%s' found in disk boot sector starting at the address
%04x\n",patterns[i].name,j-k+1);
            break;
         }
         patterns_discovered++;
      }
   }
}


void complete_search_file(file)
char file[];
{
   register int k,i;
   static int j,fd,bytes_read,bytes_in_pattern;
   static int tot_bytes;
   static unsigned char *pattern;
   static long int byte_number;

   printf("Checking %s\n",file);

   if((fd=open(file,O_RDONLY))==EOF){
      printf("Could not open file %s\n",file);
      err++;
      return;
   }

   for(byte_number=0l;;){
      switch(bytes_read=read(fd,buff+OVERLAP,BUFSIZE)){

      case 0:     /* EOF */
         break;
      case -1:
         printf("Could not read file %s\n",file);
         err++;
         return;
      default:
         tot_bytes=bytes_read+OVERLAP;
         for(k=OVERLAP;k<tot_bytes;k++){
            for(i=0;i<max_patterns;i++){

               pattern=patterns[i].pattern;

               if(pattern[0]!=buff[k]) continue;
```

```
                   if(pattern[1]!=buff[k-1]) continue;

                   bytes_in_pattern=patterns[i].bytes_in_pattern;

                   for(j=2;j<bytes_in_pattern;j++)
                       if(pattern[j]!=buff[k-j]) break; /* not there */
                   if(j<bytes_in_pattern) continue; /* not there */

                   if(byte_number==0l && k-OVERLAP+1<bytes_in_pattern) continue;

                   printf("Virus '%s' found in file %s starting at the address
%061x\n",patterns[i].name,file,byte_number+k-OVERLAP-bytes_in_pattern+1);
                   patterns_discovered++;
               }
            }
         byte_number+=bytes_read;
         total_bytes_searched+=bytes_read;
         for(i=0;i<OVERLAP;i++) buff[i]=buff[i+BUFSIZE]; /* copy down */
         continue;
      }
      break;
   }
   close(fd);
}


int find_dir(s)
char s[]; /* returns the directory name in s */
{
   struct dir_list *nextp,*nextpp;

   if(root.next == NULL) return FALSE;

   for(nextp = &root;nextp->next;nextp=nextp->next);
   strcpy(s,nextp->dir_path_and_name);

/* free space now */

   free(nextp->dir_path_and_name);

   for(nextpp = &root;(nextpp->next)!=nextp;nextpp=nextpp->next);

   free((char *) (nextpp->next));

   nextpp->next = NULL;
   return TRUE;
}


int read_patterns()
{
   FILE *infp;
   char s[MAX_LINE];

/* put in in-built patterns */

   if((infp=fopen(SEARCH_PAT,"r"))==NULL) return NO_ERROR;

   for(;max_patterns<MAX_PATTERNS;){
     switch(fmaxgets(infp,s,MAX_LINE)){
     case EOF:
        fclose(infp);
        return NO_ERROR;
```

```
       case ERROR:
         printf("Pattern string too long:\n%s\n",s);
         return ERROR;
     }
     pattern_line++; /* read from the file */
     if(contains_no_pattern(s)) continue;
     if(convert_to_pattern(&patterns[max_patterns++],s)==ERROR) return ERROR;
  }

  printf("Too many patterns in file %s\n",SEARCH_PAT);
  return ERROR;

}


int convert_to_pattern(pattp,s)
struct patt *pattp;
char s[];
{

/* this will convert the pattern in char s[] into the struct *pattp */

  register int i;
  static int noname=0;

  if(s[0]=='\0'){
     printf("Illegal zero pattern in line %d\n",pattern_line);
     return ERROR;
  }

  if(s[0]==' ' || s[0]=='\t'){ /* pattern has no name */
     sprintf(pattp->name,"Noname %d",noname++);
     i=0;
  } else{ /* get name of the pattern */
     for(i=0;i<MAX_NAME && s[i] && s[i]!=' ' && s[i]!='\t';i++)
        pattp->name[i]=(s[i]=='_'?' ':s[i]);
     if(i==MAX_NAME){
        printf("Name too long in '%s'\n",s);
        return ERROR;
     }
     pattp->name[i]='\0';
  }

  if(convert_string_to_pattern(pattp,s+i)==ERROR) return ERROR;
  return NO_ERROR;
}


int convert_string_to_pattern(pattp,s)
struct patt *pattp;
char s[];
{
  register int i,j,c,sum;

  pattp->bytes_in_pattern=0;

  for(i=j=sum=0;;){

     for(;s[i] && (s[i]==' ' || s[i]=='\t');i++); /* ffnb */
     if(s[i]=='\0' || s[i]==';'){
        if(j==1){
           pattp->pattern[pattp->bytes_in_pattern++]=sum;
        }
```

```
         if(pattp->bytes_in_pattern<2){
            printf("Illegal pattern in input line %d, '%s';\nmust have at least 2
bytes.\n",pattern_line,s);
            return ERROR;
         }
         invert_pattern(pattp->bytes_in_pattern,pattp->pattern);
         return NO_ERROR;
      }
      if((c=ishexdigit(s[i]))<0){
         printf("Spurious character %c in '%s'\n",s[i],s);
         return ERROR;
      }
      if(pattp->bytes_in_pattern>MAX_PATTERN_LENGTH){
         printf("Pattern longer than %d bytes in '%s'\n",MAX_PATTERN_LENGTH,s);
         return ERROR;
      }

      switch(j++){
      case 0:    /* first digit */
         sum=c;
         break;
      case 1:
         sum=16*sum+c;
         pattp->pattern[pattp->bytes_in_pattern++]=sum;
         j=0;
         break;
      }
      i++;
   }
}


void invert_pattern(n,s)
int n;
unsigned char s[];
{
   register int i,j,temp;

   for(i=0,j=n-1;i<n/2;i++,j--){
      temp=s[i];
      s[i]=s[j];
      s[j]=temp;
   }
}


int ishexdigit(c)
int c;
{
   switch(c){
   case '0': return 0;
   case '1': return 1;
   case '2': return 2;
   case '3': return 3;
   case '4': return 4;
   case '5': return 5;
   case '6': return 6;
   case '7': return 7;
   case '8': return 8;
   case '9': return 9;
   case 'a':
   case 'A': return 10;
   case 'b':
```

```
      case 'B':  return 11;
      case 'c':
      case 'C':  return 12;
      case 'd':
      case 'D':  return 13;
      case 'e':
      case 'E':  return 14;
      case 'f':
      case 'F':  return 15;
      default:return (-1);
      }
}


int fmaxgets(infp,s,max)
FILE *infp;
char s[];
int max;
{
   register int c,i;

   for(i=0;c=agetc(infp);) switch(c){
   case '\n':
      s[i]='\0';
      return i;
   case EOF:
      s[i]='\0';
      return i==0?EOF:i;
   default:
      s[i++]=c;
      if(i<max) break;
      s[max-1]='\0';
      return ERROR;
   }
}


contains_no_pattern(s)
char s[];
{
   register int i;

   if(s[0]==';') return TRUE;

   for(i=0;s[i];i++) switch(s[i]){
   case ' ':
   case '\t':
      continue;
   default:
      return FALSE;
   }
   return TRUE;
}


void stradd(s1,s2)
char *s1,*s2;
{
   for(;*s1;) s1++;
   for(;*s2;) *s1++ = *s2++;
   *s1='\0';
}
```

B.4 SEARCH CODE IN ASSEMBLY LANGUAGE

The assembly language code for SEARCH should be entered into one file called SEARCHAS.ASM. The FINGER program in appendix C can be used to verify the correctness of the code. The fingerprint for SEARCHAS.ASM is 9355E906 (remember to run FINGER with the -N option):

```
FINGER -N SEARCHAS.ASM
```

File SEARCHAS.ASM:

```
codeseg segment word public
dataseg segment byte public
assume cs:codeseg,ds:dataseg,es:dataseg,ss:dataseg
dataseg ends

;functions for aztec c

                public getfirst_
getfirst_:
                mov       bx,sp
                mov       dx,6[bx]    ; dma block address

; set dma address

                mov       ah,1AH
                int       21H

; get first file

                mov       dx,2[bx]    ; pathname pointer
                mov       cx,4[bx]    ; search attributes
                mov       ah,4EH
                int       21H

                jc        getfer
                mov       ax,0
getfer:         ret


                public getnext_
getnext_:
                mov       ah,4FH      ; Function 4FH
                int       21H

                jc        getner
                mov       ax,0
getner:         ret

                public bytesfree_
bytesfree_:
                mov       bx,sp
                push      bp
                mov       bp,2[bx]    ; pars address

                mov       dx,[bp]     ; drive
                mov       dh,0
                mov       ah,36H      ; Function 36H
                int       21H
```

```
                mov         2[bp],bx    ; available clusters
                mov         4[bp],dx    ; clusters per drive
                mov         6[bp],cx    ; bytes per sector
                mov         8[bp],ax    ; sectors per cluster

                pop         bp
                ret

                public absread_
absread_:
                mov         bx,sp
                push        bp
                mov         bp,bx       ; a copy

; read now

                mov         ax,2[bp]    ; drive
                mov         bx,4[bp]    ; dma block address
                mov         cx,6[bp]    ; number of sectors
                mov         dx,8[bp]    ; first sector number
                int         25H

                pop         bx          ; pop flags
                jc          rdfer
                mov         ax,0
rdfer:          pop         bp
                ret

                public lowdiskread_
lowdiskread_:
                mov         bx,sp
                push        bp
                mov         bp,bx       ; a copy

; read now

                mov         dx,2[bp]    ; head + drive
                mov         bx,4[bp]    ; dma block address
                mov         cx,6[bp]    ; cylinder + sector
                mov         ax,0201H    ; service 2, 1 sector only
                int         13H

                jc          rdler
                mov         ax,0
rdler:          pop         bp
                ret

                public currentdisk_
currentdisk_:
                mov         ah,19H
                int         21H
                and         ax,0FFH     ; result in al
                ret

codeseg ends
                end
```

C

'FINGER' VIRUS NON-SPECIFIC DETECTION PROGRAM

Just at this moment we are suffering a national defeat comparable to any lost military campaign, and what is more it is self-inflicted ... I think it is about time we pulled our finger out.

H.R.H. The Duke of Edinburgh, speaking to businessmen on 17th October 1961

This appendix contains the source code for a program called FINGER which produces cryptographic fingerprints for one file or a group of files.

By fingerprinting the original executable and then subsequently verifying that the fingerprint has not changed, one can detect a virus attack on the executable.

Although FINGER is quite usable as shown here, an average 'C' programmer can easily modify it to store the fingerprints into a file and check them automatically. Likewise, the speed of the DES code is not very high and offers plenty of scope for optimisation.

Another function of FINGER is to verify the correctness of the contents of source codes.

C.1 DESCRIPTION OF FINGER

FINGER is a program which produces cryptographic fingerprints for one file or a group of files. The fingerprint is produced using DES (Data Encryption Standard) in the mode described in ANSI standard X9.9.

FINGER can be used to produce fingerprints of binary files (like COM, and EXE files) or text files. When fingerprinting binary files, it is important to fingerprint every single byte, but when fingerprinting text files, certain (non-printable) characters can be skipped, without the meaning of the text changed in any way. For example, when entering the source code in C, one can type the TAB character or 8 blanks, without generally changing the meaning of the code. The only exceptions are quoted strings, where it is important to enter the blanks verbatim. When FINGER is fingerprinting files in the text mode, it will ignore any non-printable characters.

FINGER fingerprints files in binary mode by default. For example

```
FINGER *.EXE
```

will produce fingerprints for all EXE files in the current directory, for example

```
Fingerprint of SEARCH.EXE is f44b8704
Fingerprint of FINGER.EXE is dfbe5335
```

To produce fingerprints of the files used to make FINGER, type

```
FINGER -N FINGER.C DES.C
```

and you should get the following output:

```
Fingerprint of FINGER.C is b150e27d
Fingerprint of DES.C is b0ebe1a7
```

If you do not get that, the files with incorrect fingerprints have not been entered correctly. Note that both fingerprints will be wrong if the tables in DES.C have been entered incorrectly, even if FINGER.C is correct.

C.2 COMPILING FINGER

The majority of FINGER code is written in 'C', but two routines call DOS and are written in assembly language. The 'C' code can be compiled by most compilers, but it has been tested only using Aztec C. The assembly language routines, which are the same as for SEARCH, assume that they will be called from Aztec C. If you are using a different compiler, make sure that you use the correct calling procedure and preserve any registers required by the compiler. Some compiler libraries contain DOS calling routines directly from C and so the whole FINGER software can be written in C.

Some compilers (like Aztec) provide the make facility similar to Unix make. This simplifies the preparation of any software. The makefile for FINGER modules is listed below:

```
des.o: des.c
searchas.o: searchas.asm
finger.o: finger.c
```

```
FINGER=finger.o des.o searchas.o
finger: finger.exe
@echo finger made
finger.exe: $(FINGER)
ln $(FINGER) -lc
```

To compile FINGER, type

```
make finger
```

and the computer will do the rest.

C.3 FINGER CODE IN 'C'

The C code for FINGER is divided into two files called FINGER.C and DES.C. The file FINGER.C contains routines for file scanning, while the file DES.C contains an implementation of the Data Encryption Standard (DES), as defined in standard ANSI X3.92-1981. This is used for producing cryptographic checksums as defined in ANSI X9.9 standard.

FINGER also uses some code in assembly language, which is the same as the code used for SEARCH and contained in the file SEARCH.ASM. You only need to enter that file once.

File FINGER.C:

```
/*
   This program can be used to fingerprint any file
*/

#include "libc.h"

struct ms_dos_buff{
    char reserved[21]; /* for MS-DOS use on subsequent find_nexts */
    unsigned char attr; /* attribute found */
    unsigned int time;
    unsigned int date;
    unsigned int size_l; /* low size */
    unsigned int size_h; /* high size */
    char pname[13]; /* packed name */
};

#define SEARCH_MASK 0x07 /* DOS will return only files, not directories */

#define EOF (-1)
#define PARTEOF (-2)
#define NOTEOF (0)

#define FALSE (0)
#define TRUE (!FALSE)

void fingerprint(),des_init(),des_encrypt(),explain_command_line_arguments();

static int only_printable=FALSE;
```

```
main(argc,argv)
int argc;
char *argv[];
{
   register int i,j;
   static char key[8]={
      0x01,0x23,0x45,0x67,0x89,0xab,0xcd,0xef
   }; /* this should be a uniquely chosen key when calculating your fingerprints */
   struct ms_dos_buff fcb;

   des_init(key);

   if(argc>1) for(i=1;i<argc;i++){
      if(*argv[i]=='-') switch(*(argv[i]+1)){

      case 'N':
      case 'n':
         only_printable=TRUE;
         continue;

      default:
         break;

      } else{
         switch(j=getfirst(argv[i],SEARCH_MASK,&fcb)){
         case 2:
         case 18:
            printf("No file found corresponding to %s\n",argv[i]);
            continue;
         }

         for(;j==0;j=getnext()) fingerprint(fcb.pname);
         continue;
      }
      explain_command_line_arguments();
   } else explain_command_line_arguments();
}


void explain_command_line_arguments()
{
   printf("Command syntax:\n\nFINGER [-n] <file1> <file2> ... <filen>\n\n");
   printf("-n causes only printable characters to be fingerprinted.\n");
   exit(-1);
}


void fingerprint(file)
char file[];
{
   register int i;
   unsigned char buf[8],out[8];
   FILE *infp;

   if((infp=fopen(file,"r"))==NULL){
      printf("Cannot open %s\n",file);
      return;
   }

   printf("Fingerprint of %s is ",file);

   for(i=0;i<8;i++) out[i]=0x00; /* initialise forward buffer */
```

```
      for(;;) switch(get_bufferfull(infp,buf)){
      case EOF:
        fclose(infp);
        printf("%02x%02x%02x%02x\n",out[0],out[1],out[2],out[3]);
        return;

      case PARTEOF:
        for(i=0;i<8;i++) buf[i]=out[i]^buf[i];
        des_encrypt(buf);
        for(i=0;i<8;i++) out[i]=buf[i];
        fclose(infp);
        printf("%02x%02x%02x%02x\n",out[0],out[1],out[2],out[3]);
        return;

      case NOTEOF:
        for(i=0;i<8;i++) buf[i]=out[i]^buf[i];
        des_encrypt(buf);
        for(i=0;i<8;i++) out[i]=buf[i];
      }
}


int get_bufferfull(infp,buf)
FILE *infp;
unsigned char buf[];
{
   register int i,c;

   for(i=0;i<8;i++) switch(c=sp_getc(infp)){
   case EOF:
     if(i==0) return EOF; /* file length%8 == 0 */
     for(;i<8;i++) buf[i]=0x00;
     return PARTEOF; /* file length%8 != 0 */
   default:
     buf[i]=c;
     break;
   }
   return NOTEOF;
}


int sp_getc(infp)
FILE *infp;
{
   register int c;

   if(only_printable){
     for(;should_skip(c=getc(infp)););
     return c;
   } else return getc(infp);
}


int should_skip(c)
int c;
{
   return !(c==EOF || c>' ');
}
```

File DES.C:

```
/*
   This is the implementation of the Data Encryption Standard
*/

static int keyout[17][48];

void des_init(),lshift(),cypher(),des_encrypt(),des_decrypt();

void des_init(key) /* Calculation of Keys */
unsigned char *key;
{
   unsigned char c[28],d[28];
   static int pc1[56]={
      57,49,41,33,25,17, 9, 1,58,50,42,34,26,18,
      10, 2,59,51,43,35,27,19,11, 3,60,52,44,36,
      63,55,47,39,31,23,15, 7,62,54,46,38,30,22,
      14, 6,61,53,45,37,29,21,13, 5,28,20,12, 4
   };
   static int pc2[48]={
      14,17,11,24, 1, 5, 3,28,15, 6,21,10,
      23,19,12, 4,26, 8,16, 7,27,20,13, 2,
      41,52,31,37,47,55,30,40,51,45,33,48,
      44,49,39,56,34,53,46,42,50,36,29,32
   };
   static int nls[17]={
      0,1,1,2,2,2,2,2,1,2,2,2,2,2,2,1
   };
   static int cd[56],keyb[64];
   static int cnt,n=0;
   register int i,j;

   for(i=0;i<8;i++) /* Read in Key */
      for(j=0;j<8;j++) keyb[n++]=(key[i]>>j&0x01);

   for(i=0;i<56;i++) /* Permuted Choice 1 */
      cd[i]=keyb[pc1[i]-1];
   for(i=0;i<28;i++){
      c[i]=cd[i];
      d[i]=cd[i+28];
   }
   for(cnt=1;cnt<=16;cnt++){
      for(i=0;i<nls[cnt];i++){ /* Left Shifts */
         lshift(c);
         lshift(d);
      }
      for(i=0;i<28;i++){
         cd[i]=c[i];
         cd[i+28]=d[i];
      }
      for(i=0;i<48;i++) /* Permuted Choice 2 */
         keyout[cnt][i]=cd[pc2[i]-1];
   }
}


static void lshift(shft)          /* Left Shift Function */
unsigned char shft[];
{
   register int temp,i;
```

```
      temp=shft[0];
      for(i=0;i<27;i++) shft[i]=shft[i+1];
      shft[27]=temp;
}


static void cypher(r,cnt,fout)
int *r,*fout;
int cnt;
{
   static int expand[48],b[8][6],sout[8],pin[48];
   register int i,j;
   static int n,row,col,scnt;
   static int p[32]={
       16, 7,20,21,29,12,28,17, 1,15,23,26, 5,18,31,10,
        2, 8,24,14,32,27, 3, 9,19,13,30, 6,22,11, 4,25
   };
   static int e[48]={
       32, 1, 2, 3, 4, 5, 4, 5, 6, 7, 8, 9,
        8, 9,10,11,12,13,12,13,14,15,16,17,
       16,17,18,19,20,21,20,21,22,23,24,25,
       24,25,26,27,28,29,28,29,30,31,32, 1
   };
   static int s[8][64]={
   {
      14, 4,13, 1, 2,15,11, 8, 3,10, 6,12, 5, 9, 0, 7,
       0,15, 7, 4,14, 2,13, 1,10, 6,12,11, 9, 5, 3, 8,
       4, 1,14, 8,13, 6, 2,11,15,12, 9, 7, 3,10, 5, 0,
      15,12, 8, 2, 4, 9, 1, 7, 5,11, 3,14,10, 0, 6,13
   },
   {
      15, 1, 8,14, 6,11, 3, 4, 9, 7, 2,13,12, 0, 5,10,
       3,13, 4, 7,15, 2, 8,14,12, 0, 1,10, 6, 9,11, 5,
       0,14, 7,11,10, 4,13, 1, 5, 8,12, 6, 9, 3, 2,15,
      13, 8,10, 1, 3,15, 4, 2,11, 6, 7,12, 0, 5,14, 9
   },
   {
      10, 0, 9,14, 6, 3,15, 5, 1,13,12, 7,11, 4, 2, 8,
      13, 7, 0, 9, 3, 4, 6,10, 2, 8, 5,14,12,11,15, 1,
      13, 6, 4, 9, 8,15, 3, 0,11, 1, 2,12, 5,10,14, 7,
       1,10,13, 0, 6, 9, 8, 7, 4,15,14, 3,11, 5, 2,12
   },
   {
       7,13,14, 3, 0, 6, 9,10, 1, 2, 8, 5,11,12, 4,15,
      13, 8,11, 5, 6,15, 0, 3, 4, 7, 2,12, 1,10,14, 9,
      10, 6, 9, 0,12,11, 7,13,15, 1, 3,14, 5, 2, 8, 4,
       3,15, 0, 6,10, 1,13, 8, 9, 4, 5,11,12, 7, 2,14
   },
   {
       2,12, 4, 1, 7,10,11, 6, 8, 5, 3,15,13, 0,14, 9,
      14,11, 2,12, 4, 7,13, 1, 5, 0,15,10, 3, 9, 8, 6,
       4, 2, 1,11,10,13, 7, 8,15, 9,12, 5, 6, 3, 0,14,
      11, 8,12, 7, 1,14, 2,13, 6,15, 0, 9,10, 4, 5, 3
   },
   {
      12, 1,10,15, 9, 2, 6, 8, 0,13, 3, 4,14, 7, 5,11,
      10,15, 4, 2, 7,12, 9, 5, 6, 1,13,14, 0,11, 3, 8,
       9,14,15, 5, 2, 8,12, 3, 7, 0, 4,10, 1,13,11, 6,
       4, 3, 2,12, 9, 5,15,10,11,14, 1, 7, 6, 0, 8,13
   },
   {
       4,11, 2,14,15, 0, 8,13, 3,12, 9, 7, 5,10, 6, 1,
```

```
        13, 0,11, 7, 4, 9, 1,10,14, 3, 5,12, 2,15, 8, 6,
         1, 4,11,13,12, 3, 7,14,10,15, 6, 8, 0, 5, 9, 2,
         6,11,13, 8, 1, 4,10, 7, 9, 5, 0,15,14, 2, 3,12
    },
    {
        13, 2, 8, 4, 6,15,11, 1,10, 9, 3,14, 5, 0,12, 7,
         1,15,13, 8,10, 3, 7, 4,12, 5, 6,11, 0,14, 9, 2,
         7,11, 4, 1, 9,12,14, 2, 0, 6,10,13,15, 3, 5, 8,
         2, 1,14, 7, 4,10, 8,13,15,12, 9, 0, 3, 5, 6,11
    }
    };

    for(i=0;i<48;i++) expand[i]=r[e[i]-1]; /* Expansion Function */
    for(i=n=0;i<8;i++){ /* XOR Function */
       for(j=0;j<6;j++,n++) b[i][j]=expand[n]^keyout[cnt][n];
    }

/* Selection Functions */

    for(scnt=n=0;scnt<8;scnt++){
       row=(b[scnt][0]<<1)+b[scnt][5];
       col=(b[scnt][1]<<3)+(b[scnt][2]<<2)+(b[scnt][3]<<1)+b[scnt][4];
       sout[scnt]=s[scnt][(row<<4)+col];
       for(i=3;i>=0;i--){
          pin[n]=sout[scnt]>>i;
          sout[scnt]=sout[scnt]-(pin[n++]<<i);
       }
    }
    for(i=0;i<32;i++) fout[i]=pin[p[i]-1]; /* Permutation Function */
}

static int p[64]={
    58,50,42,34,26,18,10, 2,60,52,44,36,28,20,12, 4,
    62,54,46,38,30,22,14, 6,64,56,48,40,32,24,16, 8,
    57,49,41,33,25,17, 9, 1,59,51,43,35,27,19,11, 3,
    61,53,45,37,29,21,13, 5,63,55,47,39,31,23,15, 7
};
static int invp[64]={
    40, 8,48,16,56,24,64,32,39, 7,47,15,55,23,63,31,
    38, 6,46,14,54,22,62,30,37, 5,45,13,53,21,61,29,
    36, 4,44,12,52,20,60,28,35, 3,43,11,51,19,59,27,
    34, 2,42,10,50,18,58,26,33, 1,41, 9,49,17,57,25
};

void des_encrypt(input)
unsigned char *input;
{
    static unsigned char out[64];
    static int inputb[64],lr[64],l[32],r[32];
    static int fn[32];
    static int cnt,n;
    register int i,j;

    for(i=n=0;i<8;i++)
       for(j=0;j<8;j++) inputb[n++]=(input[i]>>j&0x01);

    for(i=0;i<64;i++){ /* Initial Permutation */
       lr[i]=inputb[p[i]-1];
       if(i<32) l[i]=lr[i];
       else r[i-32]=lr[i];
    }
    for(cnt=1;cnt<=16;cnt++){ /* Main Encryption Loop */
       cypher(r,cnt,fn); /* Execute Cypher Function */
```

```c
      for(i=0;i<32;i++){
         j=r[i];
         r[i]=l[i]^fn[i];
         l[i]=j;
      }
   }
   for(i=0;i<32;i++){
      lr[i]=r[i];
      lr[i+32]=l[i];
   }
   for(i=0;i<64;i++) out[i]=lr[invp[i]-1]; /* Inverse Initial Permutation */

   for(i=1;i<=8;i++)
      for(j=1;j<=8;j++) input[i-1]=(input[i-1]<<1)|out[i*8-j];
}


void des_decrypt(input)
/* this function is not used by FINGER, but is reproduced for completeness */
unsigned char *input;
{
   static unsigned char out[64];
   static int inputb[64],lr[64],l[32],r[32];
   static int fn[32];
   static int cnt,rtemp,n;
   register int i,j;

   for(i=n=0;i<8;i++)
      for(j=0;j<8;j++) inputb[n++]=(input[i]>>j&0x01);

   for(i=0;i<64;i++){               /* Initial Permutation */
      lr[i]=inputb[p[i]-1];
      if(i<32) l[i]=lr[i];
      else r[i-32]=lr[i];
   }
   for(cnt=16;cnt>0;cnt--){         /* Main Encryption Loop */
      cypher(r,cnt,fn); /* Execute Cypher Function */
      for(i=0;i<32;i++){
         rtemp=r[i];
         if(l[i]==1 && fn[i]==1) r[i]=0;
         else r[i]=(l[i]||fn[i]);
         l[i]=rtemp;
      }
   }
   for(i=0;i<32;i++){
      lr[i]=r[i];
      lr[i+32]=l[i];
   }
   for(i=0;i<64;i++) out[i]=lr[invp[i]-1]; /* Inverse Initial Permutation */

   for(i=1;i<=8;i++)
      for(j=1;j<=8;j++) input[i-1]=(input[i-1]<<1)|out[i*8-j];
}
```

D

ANTI-VIRUS SOFTWARE MANUFACTURERS AND DISTRIBUTORS

"Then it was false ?"
"As an address it was perfectly genuine, only it didn't happen to be mine."

J. Storer Clouston, The Lunatic at Large

Notes on Telephone and Fax numbers

U.K. numbers: U.K. numbers are shown as the dialling code plus the number. To dial a number from outside the U.K., dial the international code, followed by 44, followed by the number shown, omitting the leading 0. For example, if the number is 01 234 5678, from Germany you would dial 00 44 1 234 5678.

U.S.A. numbers: U.S.A. numbers are shown as the 3-digit area code plus 7-digit number. To dial a number from the U.K., dial 0101 followed by the number shown. For example, to dial 234 567 8901 from the U.K., you would dial 0101 234 567 8901. To dial a number from outside the U.K., dial the international code, followed by 1, followed by the number shown. For example, to dial the above number from the Vatican City State, you would dial 00 1 234 567 8901.

Other numbers: Other numbers are shown with the country code in brackets, followed by the number. To dial a number from the U.K., dial 010 followed by the number shown. For example, to dial the Swiss number (41) 1 234 5678 from the U.K., you would dial 010 41 1 234 5678. To dial a number from outside the U.K., dial the international code, followed by the number shown. For example, to dial the above number from France, you would dial 19 41 1 234 5678.

Absolute Security Inc., P.O.Box 399, 63 Great Road, Maynard, MA 01754, U.S.A., Tel: 508 897 1991, Fax: 508 897 0669

All Software, Frederiksvarksgade 96, 3400 Hilleroed, Denmark, Tel: (45) 2 740303, Fax: (45) 2 741044

American Computer Security Industries Inc., 112 Blue Hills Ct, Nashville, TN 37214, U.S.A., Tel: 6159 883 6741

Artronic Systems Ltd., 1-3 Haywra Crescent, Harrogate, HG1 5BG, U.K., Tel: 0423 525325

COMSEC (Computer Security and Software Protection), 5 Jabotinsky St, Ramat Gan 52520, POB 36890 Tel Aviv, Israel, Tel: (972) 3 751 8113, Fax: (973) 3 751 4045

Clurwin Pty. Ltd., 73 Kensington Road, South Yarra, Vic 3141, Australia, Tel: (61) 3 241 8002, Fax: (61) 3 826 2514

Compuclassics, 6934 Canby Street, Suite 109, Reseda, CA 91335, U.S.A., Tel: 818 705 1895

Computer Security Ltd., 18 Marine Parade, Brighton, BN2 1TL, U.K., Tel: 0273 672191, Fax: 0273 672542

Creem Computer Pty. Ltd., 105 Colin Street, West Perth 6005, Australia, Tel: (61) 9 481 5272, Fax: (61) 9481 5064

DDI (Digital Dispatch Inc.), 55 Lakeland Shores, St. Paul, MN 55043, U.S.A., Tel: 612 436 1000

DET (Data Encryption Technologies), PO Box 434, 8300 AK Emmerloord, The Netherlands, Tel: (31) 5270 18180, Fax: (31) 5270 18118

DMS (Distributed Management Systems), Stockclough Lane, Feniscowles, Blackburn, BD2 5JR, U.K., Tel: 0254 28419, Fax: 0383 851127

EliaShim Microcomputers Ltd., P.O.Box 8691, Haifa 31086, Israel, Tel: (972) 4 523601, Fax: (972) 4 528613

Gamma Security, 710 Wilshire Blvd, Suite 609, Santa Monica, CA 90401, U.S.A., Tel: 213 394 8622, Fax: 213 395 4214

Grey Matter Ltd., 2 Prigg Meadow, Asburton, TQ13 7DF, U.K., Tel: 0364 53499

IDS (International Data Security), 37-41 Gower Street, London, WC1E 6HH, U.K., Tel: 01 631 0548, Fax: 01 580 1466

ITL (Industrial Telecoms Ltd.), 207 Putney Bridge Road, London, SW15 2NY, U.K., Tel: 01 871 2669, Fax: 01 877 1495

Interpath Corporation, 4423 Theeney Street, Santa Clara, CA 95054, U.S.A.

Jerry FitzGerald and Associates, 506 Barkentine Lane, Redwood City, CA 94065-1128, U.S.A., Tel: 415 591 5676, Fax: 415 593 9316

LLBC Data Consult AB, 27010 Skivarp, Sweden

Lasertrieve Inc., 395 Main Street, Metuchen, NJ 08840, U.S.A., Tel: 201 906 1901, Fax: 201 985 0663

Manx Software Systems Inc., PO Box 55, Shrewsbury, NJ 07701, U.S.A., Tel: 201 542 2121

MHP, PO Box 21055, 6369 Simpelveld, The Netherlands, Tel: (31) 45 441535, Fax: (31) 45 444747

PC Security, The Old Court House, Trinity Road, Marlow, SL7 3AN, U.K., Tel: 0628 890390, Fax: 0628 890116

Panda Systems, 801 Wilson Road, Wilmington, DE 19803, U.S.A., Tel: 302 764 4722

Park Guardian Ltd., 508-514 Market Towers, 1 Nine Elms Lane, London, SW8 5NQ, U.K., Tel: 01 720 8715, Fax: 01 622 4706

Prime Factors Inc., 1470 East 20th Avenue, Eugene, OR 97403, U.S.A., Tel: 503 345 4334, Fax: 503 345 6818

Quaid Software Ltd., 45 Charles Street East, 3rd Floor, Toronto, Ontario, Canada M4Y 1S2, Tel: 416 961 8243, Fax: 416 961 6448

RG Software Systems, 2300 Computer Avenue, Suite I-51, Willow Grove, PA 19090, U.S.A., Tel: 215 659 5300, Fax: 215 886 7167

RSA Data Security Inc., 10 Twin Dolphin Drive, Redwood City, CA 94065, U.S.A., Tel: 415 595 8782, Fax: 415 595 1873

Ross Greenberg, 594 Third Avenue, New York, NY 10016, U.S.A., Tel: 212 889 6431

SA Software, 28 Denbigh Road, London, W13 8NH, U.K., Tel: 01 998 2351

S&S Enterprises, Weylands Court, Water Meadow, Germain Street, Chesham, HP5 1LP, U.K., Tel: 0494 791900, Fax: 0494 791602

Skanditek A/S, PO Box 1595 Vika, 0118 Oslo, Norway, Tel: (47) 2 206018, Fax: (47) 2 334071

Softim, Eisenauerweg 1, 7000 Stuttgart 80, West Germany, Tel: (49) 711 687 4810

Software Services, Niederwiesstrasse 8, CH-5417 Untersiggenthal, Switzerland, Tel: (41) 56 281116

Sophco Inc., P.O.Box 7430, Boulder, CO 80306, U.S.A., Tel: 303 444 1542, Fax: 303 444 1454

Sophos Ltd., Haddenham, Aylesbury, HP17 8JD, U.K., Tel: 0844 292392, Fax: 0844 291409

Sypro, Gloucester Trading Estate, Hucclecote, Gloucester, GL3 4AE, U.K., Tel: 0452 371044, Fax: 0452 613135

The Peripheral People Pty. Ltd., 41 Rawson Street, Epping, NSW 2121, Australia, Tel: (61) 2 868 4333, Fax: (61) 2 869 8259

Uti-Maco Software, Oder Weg 52-54, Frankfurt am Main, West Germany, Tel: (49) 69 590681

V Communications Inc., 3031 Tisch Way, Suite 802, San Jose, CA 95128, U.S.A., Tel: 408 296 4224

Walsham Contracts Ltd., 58 Brighton Road, Shoreham-by-Sea, BN43 6RG, U.K., Tel: 0273 597115, Fax: 0273 870020

WorldWide Software Inc, 40 Exchange Place, 15th Floor, New York, NY 10005, U.S.A., Tel: 212 422 4100, Fax: 212 422 5296

Zortech Inc., 366 Mass Ave., Arlington, MA 02174, U.S.A., Tel: 617 646 6703

Zortech Ltd., 106-108 Powis Street, London, SE18 6LU, U.K., Tel: 01 316 7777

E

GLOSSARY OF TERMS

In the beginning and in the end the only decent definition is
tautology: man is man, woman woman and tree tree.

Louis MacNeice, Plain Speaking

Access Control: Access control is the process whereby use of a computer is constrained to individual authorised users.

Add-on Card: Add-on Card means the same as PC Card.

Algorithm: Algorithms are sets of rules which specify a method of performing a task such as encryption.

ASCII: ASCII (American Standard Code for Information Interchange) is the standard system for representing letters and symbols within a computer system. Each letter or symbol is assigned a unique number between 0 and 255, which can be represented with 1 byte. ASCII code is almost universally used in non-IBM environments (IBM mainframe computers use EBCDIC code).

ANSI: ANSI (American National Standards Institute Inc.) is the organisation which issues standards in the U.S.A.

Audit Trail: Audit trails provide a date- and time-stamped record of computer usage. They record what a computer was used for, allowing a security manager to monitor the users' actions.

Authentication: Authentication is a process for verifying the correctness of a piece of data. In the case of a message it is used to verify that the message has arrived exactly as it was sent, from the person who claims to have sent it.

Background Operation: Background operation is the name applied to a program running in a multitasking environment over which the user has no direct control. To control a background operation, the user must bring it to the foreground, using operating system commands. There may be several background operations running, but only one foreground operation.

Bad Sectors: During formatting of disks, all sectors are checked for usability. Unusable sectors are 'flagged' as bad and are not used by DOS. The remaining areas can then still be used. Bad sectors are sometimes used by viruses to store the code outside the reach of the users and the operating system.

.BAT: .BAT is the extension given to 'batch' files in MS-DOS. A batch file contains a series of MS-DOS commands, which can be executed by using the name of the file as a command. AUTOEXEC.BAT is a special batch file which is executed whenever a PC is switched on, and can be used to configure the PC to a user's requirements.

Baud Rate: Baud rate is the measure of the speed of serial communications. A baud is equal to one signal element per second. Baud rate is usually expressed in bits per second (but only when one signal element equals one bit). Typical baud rates are 300, 1200, 2400 and 9600. See also serial comms and RS-232.

BIOS: BIOS (Basic Input/Output System) is that part of MS-DOS which customises the operating system to a particular machine. IBM-PCs have established a de-facto BIOS standard, so that every true compatible has to emulate the functioning of the IBM-PC BIOS.

Binary: Binary is a number system with base 2. The binary digits (Bits) are 0 and 1. Binary arithmetic is used by today's computers as the two digits 0 and 1 can be represented with two electrical or magnetic states, for example the presence and absence of a current.

Bit: A bit is the smallest unit of information, which can be either 1 or 0. The name is derived from the first and last letters of the phrase Binary Digit.

Boot Virus: A boot virus is a type of computer virus which modifies one or more of those parts of the operating system which are read in during the bootstrapping (or starting) process. Typical points of attack of a boot virus are the disk bootstrap sector and the partition bootstrap sector.

Bootstrapping: Bootstrapping means starting a computer system. 'Cold boot' means complete re-starting after switching the power on, while 'Warm boot' means partial re-starting under operating system control.

Bootstrap Sector: The bootstrap sector is that part of the operating system which is first read into memory from disk when a PC is switched on, and then loads the rest of the operating system into memory from the system files on disk. Hard disk PCs first read the contents of the disk bootstrap sector: this loads the partition bootstrap sector, which in turn loads the system files.

BSI: BSI (British Standards Institute) is the organisation issuing standards in the U.K.

Bulletin Board: Bulletin Board Systems (BBS) are computers run for electronic exchange of information. Users can access the BBS via a modem, leave and collect messages as well as download programs.

Byte: A byte is a set of 8 bits, the amount of information sufficient to store one character. It is usually the smallest individual unit that can be read from or written to PC memory.

Checksum: Checksumming is a method of detecting changes to data. Simple checksums usually involve adding or performing an exclusive-or operation on all bytes of the data. Simple checksums are not as secure as Cyclic Redundancy Checks or cryptographic checksums.

Ciphertext: Ciphertext is a term used to describe text (or data) that has been encrypted - see encryption.

CMOS: Complementary Metal Oxide Semiconductor is a technology used to manufacture chips which have very low consumption. CMOS chips are used in battery-backed applications like the time-of-day clock and the parameter memory in IBM-ATs.

.COM: .COM is the extension given to certain executable files (programs) in MS-DOS. These are similar to .EXE files, but can only contain up to 64 Kbytes of code and data. In operating systems other than DOS, the extension .COM can have a different significance.

Computer virus: See Virus.

CPU: The CPU (Central Processing Unit) is the 'heart' of every computer. It is the device which takes instructions from memory and executes them. In most PCs it is a single microprocessor.

CRC: A CRC (Cyclic Redundancy Check) is a mathematical method for verifying the integrity of data. It is a form of checksum, based on the theory of maximum-length polynomials. While more secure than a simple checksum, CRCs do not offer true cryptographic security.

Cryptographic Checksum: Cryptographic checksums use a strong cryptographic algorithm and an encryption key to produce a checksum from data. In contrast with normal checksums or CRCs, it is impossible to 'engineer' changes to data in such a way as to leave a cryptographic checksum unchanged.

Deciphering: Deciphering means the same as decrypting - see Decryption.

Decryption: Decryption is the process of transforming cipher text back into readable text; it is the reverse of encryption.

DES: DES (United States National Bureau of Standards Data Encryption Standard) is a secure algorithm for encrypting or decrypting 64 bits of data on the basis of a 56-bit key. DES is very widely used, particularly in the banking world.

Device driver: A device driver is the program which is used to 'handle' a hardware device like the screen, disk, keyboard etc. This allows the operating system to use the device without knowing specifically how the device performs a particular task.

Digital Signature: Digital signatures are checksums that depend on all the bits of a transmitted message, and also on a secret key, but which can be be checked without knowledge of the secret key.

Disk controller: A disk controller in PCs is the hardware (normally a card) which controls the operation of floppy and hard disks.

DOS: DOS (Disk Operating System) - see MS-DOS.

EEPROM: An EEPROM (Electrically Erasable Programmable Read-Only Memory, pronounced 'ee-ee-prom') is a non-volatile memory which can be written to and read from many times. It is erased by an electrical pulse. EEPROMs are used for storing data which does not change frequently, for instance setup parameters.

EFT: EFT (Electronic Funds Transfer) is a method used by banks to automate payments. Instead of writing and sending cheques, payment instructions are transmitted and processed electronically.

Electromagnetic Radiation: Electromagnetic radiation is the emission of electromagnetic waves (e.g. radio waves, microwaves etc.) from a source. It is possible to detect such radiation and extract usable information from it. The screen is the main source of electromagnetic radiation on a PC.

Electronic Mail: Electronic mail comprises messages exchanged over a computer communications network.

Enciphering: Enciphering means the same as encrypting - see Encryption.

Encryption: Encryption is the process of disguising information so that it cannot be understood by an unauthorised person. Modern encryption techniques perform their scrambling using an encryption key chosen from a very large number of possibilities.

EPROM: EPROM (Electrically Programmable Read-Only Memory) is a non-volatile memory which can be programmed (written to) once and read from many times. Most types of EPROMS can be erased by exposure to ultraviolet light. EPROMs are used for storing data which is unlikely to be changed.

.EXE: .EXE is the extension given to executable files (programs) in MS-DOS. These are similar to .COM files, but can contain more than 64 Kbytes of code and data.

Expanded memory: Memory in PCs which conforms to the industry standard specification EMS (Expanded Memory Specification) 4.0 and enables you to access more than 640K of total memory.

Extended memory: Memory in PCs which lies above 1MByte in a 80286 or 80386 machine. Extended memory is most useful in the OS/2 environment, but has limited use in the MS-DOS environment.

FAT: The File Allocation Table is a part of the operating system data which records the physical location of files on disk.

Foreground operation: Foreground operation is the name applied to a program running in a multitasking environment which the user can control by entering commands via the keyboard or the mouse.

Hardware: Any component of a computer system that has physical form. It is a term used to draw a distinction between the computer (hardware), and the programs which are executed on the computer (software).

Hexadecimal: Hexadecimal is a number system with base 16. The hexadecimal digits are represented as 0, 1, 2, 3, 4, 5, 6, 7, 8, 9, A, B, C, D, E and F. It is often used to represent binary streams, since, conveniently, each hexadecimal digit represents four bits. 0 hex represents 0000 binary, 1 hex represents 0001 binary etc until E hex which represents 1110 binary and F hex which represents 1111 binary (or 15 decimal).

Hex pattern: Hexadecimal (hex) pattern is a sequence of bytes normally used for detecting computer viruses. Commonly, patterns of 10 to 16 bytes, known to be part of a particular virus, are used.

ID: ID means an identification code, username, identification card or an identification token.

Interrupt: Interrupts are signals generated by hardware or software which alert the processor that something (usually of high priority) needs to be done. In 8088 family of processors (used by MS-DOS) interrupts cause the execution of code the address of which is stored in the 'interrupt table'. The interrupt table is located at the beginning of the RAM, in locations 0000:0000 to 0000:0400. Each interrupt address consists of 4 bytes, giving the segment address and the location within the segment.

I/O Port: A computer communicates with the outside world through I/O Ports (Input / Output Ports) e.g. RS232, printer etc.

ISO: ISO (International Organization for Standardization) is the worldwide federation of international standards bodies.

K: K is computer short-hand for 1024 (2 to the power of 10, approximately 1000). For example, 64 K or 64 Kbytes means 64 * 1024 (= 65536) bytes.

Key: Key, when used in conjunction with encryption, means a word, phrase or number on the basis of which the encryption algorithm transforms plaintext data into encrypted data or vice versa. The key is sometimes incorrectly called a password. Confusingly, key can also refer to a physical token which gives access to a system.

Key-encrypting Key: A key-encrypting key is a term used for an encryption key the sole purpose of which is to encrypt another encryption key for secure storage or transmission.

LAN: A LAN (Local Area Network) is a set of computers that can communicate with each other, usually via a cable linking them together.

Logic Bomb: A logic bomb is a program modification which causes damage when triggered by some condition such as the date, or the presence or absence of data such as a name.

MAC: A MAC (Message Authentication Code) is a cryptographic checksum for a message. Unlike a digital signature, a MAC requires knowledge of a secret key for verification.

Microprocessor: A microprocessor is the system element in control of the operation of a PC. A microprocessor reads instructions (the program) from the memory of the PC and executes the instructions.

Modem: A modem is a device which allows a PC's serial port to be connected to the telephone line. The PC can then communicate with other computers by telephone. The word modem is derived from MOdulate-DEModulate.

MS-DOS: MS-DOS is a microcomputer operating system designed by Microsoft, now virtually a de-facto standard in PCs. Its special implementation is PC-DOS, which is the operating system for IBM PCs.

Multitasking: The ability of a computer to divide its processing time among several different tasks. Although most computers contain only one processing unit, they can switch between operations so quickly that several operations may appear to run simultaneously.

Non-volatile Memory: Memory chips which retain their contents even when their normal power source is switched off. The main types are ROM, EPROM, EEPROM and battery-backed RAM.

OEM: OEM (Original Equipment Manufacturer) is the term for manufacturers who custom-label their products, which are then resold as third party products.

On-the-fly: On-the-fly encryption means that data is encrypted just before it is written to the disk, and decrypted after it has been read from the disk. Software for on-the-fly encryption can be simple to use as it is often transparent to the user.

OS: OS (Operating System) is the program which performs basic housekeeping functions in a computer system such as maintaining lists of files, running programs etc. Microcomputer operating systems include MS-DOS, Concurrent CP/M and OS/2, while minicomputer and mainframe operating systems include Unix, VMS and MVS.

OS/2: OS/2 is an operating system for 80286 and 80386 based microcomputers. It is multitasking (several applications can be executed at the same time).

.OVL: .OVL is the extension given to overlay files (programs) in MS-DOS. Overlay files are used with large programs which cannot all fit into RAM at the same time. Parts of the program (overlays) are loaded only when needed.

Parasitic virus: A parasitic virus is a type of computer virus which attaches itself to another program and is activated when that program is executed. A parasitic virus can either append itself to the end of a program (in which case the program functionality is normally preserved) or overwrite a part of the program (in which case the program functionality is destroyed).

Partition record: Partition record is the first sector found on IBM-PC hard disks which contains information about the disk like the number of sectors per partition. This record also contains the code which is executed when the PC is bootstrapped.

Password: Passwords are sequences of characters which allow users access to part of a system. Although they are supposed to be unique, experience has shown that most people's choices are highly insecure, tending to choose short words such as names, which are easy to guess.

PC: A PC (Personal Computer) is a desktop or portable single-user computer usually consisting of a screen, keyboard, disk drives and the processing unit.

PC Card: PC Cards are often installed in personal computers (PCs) to enhance the capability of the computer. They are usually placed in one of several slots available within the hardware of the PC. Examples include internal modems, graphics cards and expanded memory.

PC-DOS: PC-DOS is the Microsoft microcomputer operating system used by IBM in its highly successful series of PCs. PC-DOS is a customised version of MS-DOS which is used by IBM compatibles.

Peripheral: Peripherals are devices externally connected to a computer, such as a printer or a plotter. Examples of peripherals include compact disk drives, external modems, the mouse and external disk drives.

PIN: PIN - Personal Identification Number. A sequence of digits used to verify the identity of the holder of a token. A kind of password.

Pixel: Pixels are tiny elements that form a digitised picture, for example on a computer screen. Each pixel represents a degree of brightness and colour assigned to that point in the picture.

Plaintext: Plaintext is the opposite of ciphertext. It comprises text or data in normally readable form rather than encrypted.

Plug-in Card: Plug-in Card means the same as PC Card.

Program: Programs are precise sequences of instructions that specify what action a PC should perform. Computer programs are often called software.

PS/2: PS/2 is the new series of microcomputers from IBM which are designed to replace the PC/XT/AT range. All models, except model 30, support the 'microchannel architecture'. Cards designed for the IBM PC/XT/AT are not compatible with PS/2 machines (with the exception of PS/2 Model 30).

Public Key: A public key is a cryptographic key which can be used to encrypt but is not capable of decryption. See also RSA.

RAM: RAM (Random Access Memory) is the volatile memory in a computer system which can be accessed very quickly. It can both be written to and read from. It is usual to 'load' programs which will be executed from disk into RAM and then execute them. The operating system takes care of the allocation of RAM to executing programs.

Risk Analysis: Risk analysis is the analysis of a system's assets and vulnerabilities in an attempt to establish the expected loss when a given disaster occurs.

ROM: ROM (Read Only Memory) is the non-volatile memory in a computer system. Data is embedded into it during manufacture. It is usually used to store the starting code which is executed by the PC on power up (see bootstrapping).

RS-232: RS-232 is a very widely used standard for serial data communication over short distances (up to approximately 100 metres). The speed of communication is measured in baud. See also serial comms.

RSA: RSA is the encryption algorithm invented by Rivest, Shamir and Adleman in 1976. It uses different keys for encryption and for decryption: it is a 'public key' or 'asymmetric' algorithm.

Secret Key: Secret Keys are encryption keys that must not be disclosed. If they are revealed, the security offered by an encryption algorithm is compromised. Not all encryption keys have to be kept secret, see Public Key.

Security Manager: Security Managers are staff charged with the setting up and subsequent monitoring of a security system. They often have special rights of access, and can introduce or remove users. Because he has special powers, a security manager must be trusted to carry out his job.

Serial Comms: Serial communication is a way of transmitting data using only one pair of wires, compared with the many wires needed for parallel communication. This simplicity is compensated by a lower throughput than parallel communications. See also RS-232.

Server: A network computer that provides files and/or devices (e.g. printers) which can be shared by workstations connected to the network. The server normally has a large disk drive which acts as a file depository for everybody on the network. Since all files are stored in a central location, file sharing is easier.

Software: See Program.

.SYS: .SYS is the extension given to system files in MS-DOS. System files are sometimes 'Hidden' so that they do not appear in directory listings. A typical example is the configuration file CONFIG.SYS, which sets up various configuration parameters for the operating system on power-up, as well as the files containing MS-DOS itself.

Token: A token is a physical object, sometimes containing sophisticated electronics, which is used to gain access to a system. Some tokens contain a microprocessor and are called 'intelligent tokens'.

Trojan Horse: A Trojan horse is a program which causes a security breach by performing services beyond those stated in its specifications. The effects can be (and often are) malicious.

TSR: TSR (Terminate and Stay Resident) is a term for MS-DOS programs which remain in memory after being executed. They can be re-activated either by a specific sequence of keystrokes, or at some specific time, or by some specific signal from an I/O port.

Unix: Unix is a multi-user computer operating system developed at Bell Laboratories in the U.S.A. Programs written for Unix are usually portable from one computer model to another. Several versions exist, with Unix 3 and Unix 5 being popular on minicomputers. Xenix, a close relative of Unix, is popular on PCs.

Virus: A virus, or a computer virus, is a program which makes copies of itself in such a way as to 'infect' parts of the operating system and/or application programs. See also 'Parasitic virus' and 'Boot virus'.

Virus signature: Virus signature is an identifier recognised by the virus as meaning 'this item is already infected, do not reinfect'. It can take different forms like the text 'sURIV' (VIRUs spelled backwards) or the size of the file divisible by a certain number.

Volatile Memory: Memory chips which forget their contents when their normal power source is switched off. The main type of volatile memory is the RAM used as the main memory of a computer.

Worm: A program similar to a computer virus, and often confused with it. Unlike a computer virus, which propagates by attaching itself to other programs, a worm usually exists as a program in its own right. Worms spread by manipulation of electronic mail or similar facilities.

F

ASCII CHARACTERS

> He intended, he said, to devote the rest of his life to learning the
> remaining twenty-two letters of the alphabet.
>
> *George Orwell, Animal Farm*

The two tables which follow list the characters as defined by the ASCII code (ASCII is the acronym for "American Standard Code for Information Interchange").

Note that the US version of the code is shown and that in the UK the hash symbol (#) (ASCII value 35 Decimal) is usually printed as the pound sign.

The characters with values from 0 to 31 Decimal are the so called 'control characters' and do not correspond to any printable symbols. They are usually available on the keyboard by keeping the Control (Ctrl) key pressed and typing a character. As most of them have a special significance, their name is also given; for example Control L is 'Form Feed', Control [is 'Escape' etc.

Control (non-printable) characters are shown in the first table, while the printable characters are shown in the second table.

Control (non-printable) ASCII characters

Control characters are shown preceded by '^'. For example, Control A is shown
as '^A' and Control D as '^D'.

Decimal	Hex	Character	Name
00	00	^@	NUL (Null)
01	01	^A	SOH (Start of heading)
02	02	^B	STX (Start of text)
03	03	^C	ETX (End of text)
04	04	^D	EOT (End of transmission)
05	05	^E	ENQ (Enquiry)
06	06	^F	ACK (Acknowledge)
07	07	^G	BEL (Bell)
08	08	^H	BS (Backspace)
09	09	^I	HT (Horizontal TAB)
10	0a	^J	LF (Line feed)
11	0b	^K	VT (Vertical TAB)
12	0c	^L	FF (Form feed)
13	0d	^M	CR (Carriage return)
14	0e	^N	SO (Shift out)
15	0f	^O	SI (Shift in)
16	10	^P	DLE (Data link escape)
17	11	^Q	DC1 (Device control 1, XON)
18	12	^R	DC2 (Device control 2)
19	13	^S	DC3 (Device control 3, XOFF)
20	14	^T	DC4 (Device control 4)
21	15	^U	NAK (Negative acknowledge)
22	16	^V	SYN (Synchronous idle)
23	17	^W	ETB (End of transmitted block)
24	18	^X	CAN (Cancel line)
25	19	^Y	EM (End of medium)
26	1a	^Z	SUB (Substitute)
27	1b	^[	ESC (Escape)
28	1c	^\	FS (File separator)
29	1d	^]	GS (Group separator)
30	1e	^^	RS (Record separator)
31	1f	^_	US (Unit separator)

Printable ASCII characters

Dec	Hex	Char	Dec	Hex	Char	Dec	Hex	Char
32	20	(SPACE)	64	40	@	96	60	'
33	21	!	65	41	A	97	61	a
34	22	"	66	42	B	98	62	b
35	23	#	67	43	C	99	63	c
36	24	$	68	44	D	100	64	d
37	25	%	69	45	E	101	65	e
38	26	&	70	46	F	102	66	f
39	27	'	71	47	G	103	67	g
40	28	(	72	48	H	104	68	h
41	29	)	73	49	I	105	69	i
42	2a	*	74	4a	J	106	6a	j
43	2b	+	75	4b	K	107	6b	k
44	2c	,	76	4c	L	108	6c	l
45	2d	-	77	4d	M	109	6d	m
46	2e	.	78	4e	N	110	6e	n
47	2f	/	79	4f	O	111	6f	o
48	30	0	80	50	P	112	70	p
49	31	1	81	51	Q	113	71	q
50	32	2	82	52	R	114	72	r
51	33	3	83	53	S	115	73	s
52	34	4	84	54	T	116	74	t
53	35	5	85	55	U	117	75	u
54	36	6	86	56	V	118	76	v
55	37	7	87	57	W	119	77	w
56	38	8	88	58	X	120	78	x
57	39	9	89	59	Y	121	79	y
58	3a	:	90	5a	Z	122	7a	z
59	3b	;	91	5b	[	123	7b	{
60	3c	<	92	5c	\	124	7c		
61	3d	=	93	5d	]	125	7d	}
62	3e	>	94	5e	^	126	7e	~

INDEX

Index, I copy from old Vladivostok telephone directory ...

Tom Lehrer, "Lobachevsky"